THE SERGEANT MAJOR SYNDROME

THE
SERGEANT MAJOR
S Y N D R O M E

A BOOK FOR PEOPLE WHO WANT TO ADVANCE THEIR CAREERS

ROY JACQUES with MARY HOBSON

www.sergeantmajorsystems.com

"For you suffer fools gladly, seeing yourself as wise."
- II Corinthians 11:19.

OPEN BOOK
EDITIONS
A Berrett–Koehler Partner

The Sergeant Major Syndrome
A Book for People Who Want to Advance Their Careers

iUniverse books may be ordered through booksellers or by contacting:

iUniverse
1663 Liberty Drive
Bloomington, IN 47403
www.iuniverse.com
1-800-Authors (1-800-288-4677)

Because of the dynamic nature of the Internet, any web addresses or links contained in this book may have changed since publication and may no longer be valid. The views expressed in this work are solely those of the author and do not necessarily reflect the views of the publisher, and the publisher hereby disclaims any responsibility for them.

Any people depicted in stock imagery provided by Thinkstock are models, and such images are being used for illustrative purposes only.

Certain stock imagery © Thinkstock.

ISBN: 978-1-4620-2207-6 (sc)
ISBN: 978-1-4620-2209-0 (hc)
ISBN: 978-1-4620-2208-3 (e)

Library of Congress Control Number: 2011914640

Printed in the United States of America

iUniverse rev. date: 09/19/2011

TABLE OF CONTENTS

PART ONE: SERGEANT MAJORS, ATTEN-TION!

⌒⋎⌒

In the glory days of the British Empire, commissioned officers in the military were children of the aristocracy. A commoner entering the ranks might hope to rise to the rank of Sergeant Major (Master Sergeant), but there was no chance of crossing the glass ceiling separating the enlisted men from the commissioned officers, Lieutenant and above. It was widely known that the British army was run by its Sergeant Majors, but, no matter how much a Sergeant Major was valued, the reward for performing well was no more than another seniority stripe on his sleeve and another, more impossible assignment. Those who lived to retire ended their careers with Her Majesty's sincerest gratitude— and little else.

I have served as a corporate Sergeant Major and, if you are reading this book with interest, then probably so have you. Unlike our military predecessor, today's organizational Sergeant Major is not held down by tradition or policy, but by a variety of factors which, if understood, can be changed. Part One of this book will help you to understand what a Sergeant Major is and how these limiting factors operate. In Part Two, we outline a plan for strategizing what you will choose to do about being—or not being— a Sergeant Major.

CHAPTER 1:
I HAVE BEEN A SERGEANT MAJOR; HAVE YOU?

cm

The inspiration for this book came to me about a decade ago when I was chatting with a group of people who, like me, were unemployed. We were having coffee in the offices of Forty Plus, an organization dedicated to helping older, unemployed people find jobs. A casual conversation with two others had turned to the topic of how difficult it is to get on politically in organizations. After all, we agreed, we work hard and do good work. Why should we have to deal with that "bullshit"? Susan mentioned once having been told that she "doesn't suffer fools gladly". Leo and I smiled at this. It turned out that in his sales career and my software development days, we had each heard exactly those same words from our bosses.

We asked the next two people who passed through the room if they had ever been told they "didn't suffer fools gladly." Sure enough, both of them had. In fact, without exception, we all not only recognized the phrase, it inspired each of us to gleefully tell a story about a time when we had put such a fool in their place.

Discovering the Sergeant Major

That's when a thought first crossed my mind: Was it just a coincidence that the five of us were having career trouble in the hottest economy the state had ever seen? In my case, I had been able to turn four university degrees, three decades of experience and an impressive amount of hard work into surprisingly little. The "fools" we had not suffered gladly were still working. Many of them had been promoted and, hell, they had been our bosses to begin with! Who was suffering and who were the fools?

I have given considerable thought to this because it is part of a larger question that has occupied me my entire professional and academic life: why is it that in every place I have worked, the people I most value usually seem to get sidelined, while I see the people who rise rapidly in the organization as— to be very merciful— less outstanding? As I began to think more about this phenomenon, I realized how many people I knew who were sidelined in this fashion. I began to call this group Sergeant Majors because, like our namesake in the old British army, we were valued as long as we followed orders, but we were very unlikely to join the group giving the orders.

How, I wondered, do Sergeant Majors become Sergeant Majors? Can organizations be managed so stupidly that they systematically select the worst people and discard the best? Even with my years of accumulated resentment, this conclusion seemed a bit extreme. As my co-author is fond of saying, when you have a problem and it has no solution, it isn't a problem; it's a fact. There are certainly bad individual organizations, incompetent individual managers and individuals who advance themselves at the expense of others. But, I began to think, if the people I admire are passed over systematically, there must be reasons I am failing to see.

In an old movie called *The Passenger*, an American reporter played by Jack Nicholson asks a question of a North African Bedouin. The Bedouin looks for a long while at the microphone Nicholson is sticking in his face before replying, "I'm sure any question you could ask me would tell me far more about you than my answer could tell you about me." That was one of my problems—my questions already contained (bad) answers. I was trying to understand the Sergeant Major syndrome while thinking as a Sergeant Major.

I began to realize that if I wanted to understand what was going on I needed to ask my question differently. To ask why organizations are run so poorly is a judgment, not a question. I realized I needed to learn to think as objectively as possible about *how* Sergeant Majors become Sergeant Majors. Here are some examples of changing the questions I asked:

> From: Why do the bullshitters and brown-nosers get ahead?
> *To: What do those who get ahead know that I don't?*

> From: Why do the best people get sidelined?
> *To: What do the people who get sidelined lack?*

> From: Why do the Sergeant Majors have to work for idiots?
> *To: How did that "idiot" get ahead of the Sergeant Major?*

Note how the earlier set of questions clearly shows the Sergeant Major in me. The questions answer themselves. They say that I am right and good and the problem is others who are ignorant and unprincipled. They say that the world is wrong for failing to listen to me. They say, quite clearly, "I'm not ready to be part of things. Put me in `special projects' or discard me in the next restructuring".

Five Key Points in This Book

Once I started asking more useful questions, I found that I could better understand the Sergeant Major Syndrome, the process by which Sergeant Majors are created, burned out and discarded. Once I began to look at the situation less judgmentally, I learned the first major lesson: ***Getting promoted is a different job from doing your job***. Sergeant Majors I have known (and been) tend to expect excellent performance of our work to lead to advancement. We tend to be surprised, and often upset, when it leads to another job of the same type. I'll return to this point in more detail in the next chapter.

My second major insight did not occur until a couple years later when I was running my own business. After having the experience of employing one or two Sergeant Majors, I came to realize, to my chagrin, that: ***Sergeant Majors often need to be contained*** *because we can disrupt organizations when we think we are being our most useful*. We are prone to put our needs above the needs of the group; and value our projects above the overall work of the organization. Our passion for doing excellent work is a double-edged sword. It often makes us excellent project leaders, but it equally often sets us against the very organization we think we are serving.

So, how does a Sergeant Major who wishes to advance in the organization better understand how to do so? Pondering this question over many years led to my third major point: **Organizations are tribal**. Yes, there are a lot of formal rules in organizations and merit is sometimes rewarded, but this isn't a game of baseball where everyone plays according to a complete set of rules, the umpire sees all and the one with the most points is declared the champion. Sure, you need to play by the rules in organizations, but you also need to know that those rules cover only a part of the game. What other rules govern the tribal part of the game? We will discuss this also.

The fourth point follows from the third: **You are playing from the wrong rule book!** You have seen evidence of the tribal organization, but you have probably called it something else. When your co-worker spent so much time chatting to the higher-ups at the company picnic, you saw it as sucking up. When you thought the head of marketing was being a jerk in that meeting, you said so right in the meeting— and justified it as honesty. When you contradicted your boss to her boss, you thought the guy who saved face by showing how you were both right, in different ways, was two-faced. In all of these things, you were playing from the rules you knew which said getting the best project outcome is the same as getting the best organizational outcome. Well, it isn't and we have to talk about this.

There is one more key point: **It's OK to be a Sergeant Major- as long as that's your choice**. Not all of us want to advance in organizations. Many will find it more satisfying to remain individual contributors or team leaders. The British Empire could not have survived without its Sergeant Majors; neither can the modern organization. Being a Sergeant Major is only a problem if you're trying to become something else. When you are locked unwillingly into this situation, a vicious circle of negative reinforcement begins that is an impediment to the welfare of the organization and, as a consequence, a greater impediment to your organizational welfare. That is the Sergeant Major Syndrome.

Whether you wish to be personally satisfied working as a Sergeant Major or you wish to become part of the organizational "officer corps", you need to understand both how a Sergeant Major can be valuable to an organization and how he or she can become an obstruction—often while being quite unaware of it. In the following pages I will describe the characteristics of a Sergeant Major and discuss many of the life influences that can produce a Sergeant Major attitude. I will then describe what the Sergeant Major can do to thrive in the tribal organization. If you wish to continue as a Sergeant Major, this information will help you to be valued at the project level and to avoid that agonizing path out the organizational side door. If you wish to advance from your present position into the officer corps, this book will help you stop pressing your face against the glass ceiling and will show you where to find the stairs.

CHAPTER 2:
ARE YOU A SERGEANT MAJOR?

What makes a Sergeant Major a Sergeant Major? After all, we don't wear service stripes or uniforms. If you have experienced problems as a Sergeant Major, the likelihood is that you have thought about them as uniquely personal issues or as problems with a particular boss or organization. The first thing you need to know if that you are not alone. There are millions of us and we have a lot in common. Look at the following list and check every box that applies to you:

☐ I am good at my job and hold myself to high standards.
☐ I achieve my goals at any cost
☐ Others don't seem to care as much as I do
☐ I tell people what I think and those who don't are inauthentic
☐ I tend to dislike those who get in my way
☐ My boss just doesn't get it
☐ Workers tend to know what's going on more than bosses
☐ I could do a better job of running this company
☐ I am unappreciated/underappreciated; I don't get what I deserve
☐ I have been told I don't suffer fools gladly
☐ I don't know why they promote the people they do
☐ I stand up for people who I think are being mistreated—regardless
☐ I get great performance evaluations; why don't I get promoted?
☐ My last several projects have been becoming more and more impossible
☐ I work best when I am left alone
☐ When people cross me, they learn to regret it

The more boxes you checked, the more you think like a Sergeant Major. First, let's acknowledge that there's a good side to being this type of employee. You are competent. You care about the work, probably passionately. You aren't just a dreamer; you're willing to do what it takes to finish the job successfully. You probably have a series of positive performance reviews to document that your dedication and ability haven't gone unnoticed.

This is why there's nothing wrong with deciding you want to remain a Sergeant Major if moving up the ladder isn't what you want. But, whether you want to become a manager or not, every Sergeant Major has to look at the dark side of this dedication to duty. If it isn't managed properly, a good Sergeant Major can come to be seen as an unreasonable, unbalanced jihadist, a problem rather than a solution. I use the term *jihad* with respect. the spiritual war of good against evil has an appropriate place in religious practice. To mistake work for a war of good against evil is another story. This is perhaps the core quality a Sergeant Major must learn to control.

Seven Signs of the Sergeant Major Syndrome

1. "It's Just Business".

The epitaph of the Sergeant Major should be, "I have standards, dammit." Up to a point, this is a good thing, but when these standards are not met, Sergeant Majors tend to see those who do not share them as the enemy. If there has been one lesson I have learned that was hard to swallow, it was recognizing that the people I support and value are, on the whole, neither better nor worse than those I have opposed. To the extent that we see co-workers in terms of good and bad, we handicap ourselves. We introduce into our work a moral dimension that does not belong there and a rigidity that makes us less effective.

There are many organizational lessons a Sergeant Major can learn from *The Godfather* movies. One of these comes after the famous scene where Sonny is so gruesomely murdered at the toll booth. "It's just business" says the heartbroken Don Corleone, refusing to go to war over it. Indeed, he calls a meeting to sue for peace. If the death of a son can be "just business" what are we working on that's so important? The more we see those in our way as evil, the more we are likely to become Sonny, a casualty of letting our passion cloud our judgment.

2. Ebony and Ivory.
Sergeant Majors tend to think in black and white terms. We tend to associate compromise with character deficiency and low product quality. If the marketing manager doesn't understand our presentation, he's "an idiot." If the head of manufacturing wants to change our design so it can be made less expensively by utilizing production steps or materials from another product she's "the enemy". We tend to dislike those with whom we disagree, so that all disagreements are colored with an aura of "for me or against me." This makes an open exchange of ideas and collaboration about mutual problems difficult.

Such an attitude tends to block the free flow of necessary information and reduces opportunities for productive collaboration across the organization. It can also lead easily into "guerrilla" tactics for getting the project done by flouting procedures, hoarding resources and otherwise promoting the "good" project over the "bad" organization. A balanced view of the work exists somewhere between right and wrong, true and false, good and bad. Thinking in either/or terms is like trying to work blindfolded.

3. Defending the Moral High Ground (Alone).
We probably don't mean to act as superior beings, but when we see those in our way as bad or wrong, rather than as other committed people with differing tasks, expertise or values; we are identifying ourselves as the Chosen of God. We place ourselves on the moral high ground. If we have difficulties and failures, it is the fault of those who have not learned that God speaks to us and us alone.

You can see why this might not appeal to others if you imagine dealing with somebody like that yourself. The moral high ground is a lonely spot. It prevents our working collaboratively with those whose vision differs from ours. There is an old saying that, "to understand is to forgive". The converse of that statement is equally true. As long as we are judging, we cannot understand. Without that understanding, how can we fit into a complex organization in which our project is only one part of a larger goal?

4. You Have a Better Plan.

You know how the company should be better run, don't you? You were talking about it within the last twenty-four hours, in the lunchroom, to your partner—to that poor woman on the bus! What's really frustrating is that you may even be right. Filling out those time recording forms really is a waste of productive time. Those endless meetings Fred calls are unnecessary. Betty and Brian really are blaming your team for things they failed to do themselves. If you were God, you really could straighten things out.

But you're not God; we were just discussing that. You are a part, probably a small part, of a much larger enterprise. For your bosses, who are looking at the organization as a whole, it is far more important that you fit in than it is that you have a brilliant blueprint for success. Imagine yourself in their position. If you did have the chance to reconfigure things according to your plan, how much authority would you assign to somebody who had their own plan showing yours to be all wrong?

This is where that word "balance" comes up again. If you have a suggestion for improving things, it may be welcomed. If your suggestion requires your bosses to admit that they're jerks or if it involves a new vision for the company, this is a sign that it's time to examine your thinking. My favourite thought from Kafka is, "it is not necessary to accept everything as true; one must only accept it as necessary". The vision, mission and plan you're working under may or may not be the best, but they are the ones you are working under. Unless you support them, you hurt yourself without helping anyone else.

5. Our Omniscient Bosses.

Paradoxically, even though nobody really understands things except us, and perhaps out team, there is a way in which we treat our bosses as if they knew everything. About the time I finished my MBA, I had an informal job interview with a person much senior to me in my organization. He and I had taken an MBA class together and had spoken at a few parties so, although I didn't work for him, we knew each other a bit. I began by saying, "Well, Peter, I think you have a pretty good idea of what I can do…" I was shocked when he interrupted me to say, "Roy, I have no idea what you do."

Unless our bosses work shoulder to shoulder with us, they only see the small portions of our work life that come to their attention. Those portions may fairly reflect our efforts and value. Then again, they may not. Those hours you spent helping the new person learn the ropes, that night you worked until two a.m. to make sure the Toronto office had the report for their breakfast meeting, the fact that you're the "go to" person for everyone in your department who has a thorny problem—all of these actions have value to the company and you're right to see them as part of the value you bring, but how visible are they? *You won't get credit for things nobody knows you did.*

The same holds true of your personnel file. Human resources knows about some of the things you've done and it has records of your performance evaluations, but these have been based on a formal process designed to look only at specific, generic items. It does not cover most details of your work day. Look at it the other way round. How much of your boss's day do you know about and how much is hidden from you? Your boss is no more omniscient than you are. Yes, you "should" get the credit you "deserve" for doing for invisible work, but you will find that when you are using the words "should" or "deserve" you are asking the world to be different than it is. It isn't.

6. Looking Downward.

Many Sergeant Majors are well liked by the people they supervise. We tend to value "our" people and care about their welfare. We may tend to ask too much of them, but we are ready to go to bat for them against "the suits". We can be proud of this orientation-up to a point. We go too far when we define ourselves as defenders of our people against management. Our job is to be a mediator between the vision and goals of management and the efforts of our people to realize those goals. When we define management as the opposition, is it any wonder we tend to stay in "special projects" instead of being asked to join the enemy?

The challenge is to remain (here it is again!) balanced in our dual allegiances to the team and the organization. That word, "balance" tends to be a problem for the Sergeant Major. We prefer things that can be maximized or minimized (more black and white thinking there). What others see as balance often looks to us like mere mediocrity.

7. Scorched-Earth Diplomacy.

What do you do when somebody blocks your way, fails to support your work, argues for a different path or just plain messes up? Are you proud of the times you've shown somebody not to mess with you? Did you burn the skin from their face with your response, put them in their place, teach them a lesson they won't soon forget? Sergeant Majors tend to like to settle differences in Thunderdome, "two men enter; one man leaves" (or one woman). What we fail to realize is that in organizations, as with countries, there are no victors in a war. Every war is a failure of diplomacy. You can be the lesser loser, but you cannot win.

The person who shows that they have the potential to advance in the organization is not the one who creates conflict, but the one who makes it go away. The person who soothes ruffled feathers, gets conflicting views on the table and arranges a negotiated truce where everyone gets part of what they were after is more likely to emerge the hero. For that matter, as long as we're thinking in terms of heroes at all, we're on the wrong page. Heroes require villains. Organizations require colleagues, not heroes and villains. Remember, your project will end someday, but the people will remain—along with the good or bad feelings your project engendered.

Two Key Points

Ok, you care about the work. You care about your team. You have thrown yourself passionately into the project and you've done well. Whether the goal was to convert the old database to a new platform, to increase purchases of Budweiser in Denver or to get the third quarter financials broken down by region for the annual meeting, you succeeded. What happens now? You probably got a pro forma pat on the head—"Thanks Roy; Nice job"—then everyone went on with their life. You probably felt a bit snubbed; they don't appreciate everything you went through to deliver the goods. Remember, though, for them this is just work, not holy war.

Ask yourself also whether the way you got the job done has caused collateral damage. Maybe your accounts receivable person resents that you got goods shipped to a client with bad credit in order to make your sales goal. Perhaps another team is upset that they were unable to get bandwidth on the mainframe computer because you intimidated the head of IT into giving your group extra usage. Oh, don't forget that product manager you told off in front of three associates because she didn't have the technical information you needed on time. Maybe there is lingering damage even on your own team—maybe from the family members you called in at last minute for the final Sunday review so everything would be ready Monday morning…

Have you considered the possibility that perhaps, as things stand, you don't deserve that promotion you want? Perhaps you *could* be effective in the position for which you were passed over, but maybe you need to think a little differently about the job and your preparation for it. There are two key points to bear in mind:

1. You have been working only on your job, not on your career.

2. Until you develop new ways of working, you are not ready to advance. If you were the company president, would you give somebody like you greater authority?

At different points in my career I have been both a Sergeant Major and an employer. Speaking as an employer, I can say unreservedly that dependability and loyalty had vastly more value to me and to my organization than did brilliance. The brilliant employee may occasionally be tolerated when his or her brilliance is needed, but that is surprisingly seldom. Brilliance is about as useful in producing organizational success as dynamite is for heating a house. Far more often, outstanding success results from outstanding coordination of ordinary efforts. Let me tell you about Nathan.

Nathan was a counter worker in my first café. He was about nineteen when I hired him. I was initially impressed that he was hard working and personable. Customers loved him. The problem was that Nathan had an IQ that was probably north of 150 and he was bored by routine. One day I came into the shop to find he had changed the jazz soundtrack we played to a local blues radio station. He made up special drinks for customers that other staff members were unable to reproduce when he wasn't at work. He would go beyond required procedures when he thought he should and neglect them when he decided they weren't useful. As much as I liked Nathan, I eventually fired him. I needed somebody who stood out _like_ the others, not somebody who stood out _from_ the others. Nathan was a Sergeant Major in the making. He did _his_ job, not _our_ job.

Let me illustrate some of these points with the lesson of my own early managerial experience. This is the story of how I first got into "special projects"—you know, the organizational limbo warehousing the people who are temporarily too valuable to fire, but not of any clear and immediate use.

Heating My House with Dynamite

After three years of glowing performance reviews and with my new MBA, I was promoted from an individual contributor position in software support to project management. It was a somewhat delicate situation, since the division to which I was transferred had been a competing company prior to being acquired in a recent merger. My team was one of three working on various financial software products. Mine was a staff position; "my" team formally answered to the line manager running software development.

In some ways, I was effective in my job. I won the respect of my team. We produced a good product that was delivered on time. I communicated effectively about this product to the sales and support staff. My performance was evaluated very favorably by my superiors. From a Sergeant Major's standpoint, I scored 100%. It might have seemed I was well positioned for a promotion to line management. Instead, however, I was "promoted" to a special projects team in which I was, once again, an individual contributor.

For a couple years I worked on less and less feasible projects until I left the company.

Yes, I was a bit bitter. I blamed organizational politics and managerial ineptitude. But, looking back, were they wrong? There is another side to my story. I had pulled my team together by emphasizing how special we were relative to the others. I was not beyond intimidating the manager of software development to get what I wanted from him. I was not well liked by the programmers who were on other teams and I was less liked by my fellow project managers. Would you have promoted me into a position where these people answered to me? Looking back, I wouldn't.

So What Else Could I Have Done?

So, what might I have done to more successfully show that I was a good candidate for my boss's job? I could have put the company first, not my team. I could have fit in better and had a more appropriate attitude toward the work. I could have demonstrated better awareness of the broader context that my boss had to consider, accepted the ambiguity and contradictions that are part of that environment and sought informal mentorship from those who operated in that environment, starting with my boss. Let me expand on this.

Promote the Company, Not the Team

Who was I working for? At the time, I would have said it was the company, but that was my misperception. I was working against the company to promote the success of my team. One way I did this was to foster a sense of our team being different from and superior to the others. One memo referred to my group as "the A Team". For anyone who remembers that old TV show, the A Team were a group of mavericks whose solution to every problem was to spray it with automatic weapons fire. Did being seen this way foster the idea that I was putting the organization's welfare ahead of the interest of my group? I doubt it.

Fitting In

There were other ways I got to my goals at the expense of the company. The group I was managing had recently been taken over by the larger company from which I had been sent. This had nominally been a merger, not a takeover, but one culture dominated the company and there was still strong "rebel" sentiment in my group. Rather than trying to build bridges and help to minimize this sense of *us/them*, I used it to my team's advantage by fostering the feeling that we would show "them" what "we" could do. In the short run, it was motivational, but if you were observing this, would you want a person who used this tactic to have authority beyond their team? Probably not.

Considering the Broader Context
A feature of this company's culture was that people with technical degrees tended to remain in technical positions. The middle layers of management were populated by nontechnical people, mostly MBAs. The highest levels of the company were predominantly people with business expertise specialized in finance. I had an MBA and work experience in the programming and customer service end of the company. This background could have been used to build bridges between the technical and business subcultures. Doing so might have demonstrated to my bosses that I was able to strengthen the company by increasing understanding between these key groups. Instead, I was prone to highlight anything management did which could be interpreted to show that they didn't understand or care about us. It was effective in creating a "we'll show them" attitude in my group, but, in the bigger picture, it worked against building an effective overall organization.

Bear in mind that I was sent to this company from "them", the people who had purchased it. I was already seen as an outsider from my first day on the job. By fanning the flames of "we/they", I may have taken the path of least resistance in showing my team I was on their side and in firing them up to show what they could do. But even as I did this, I was showing every one else in that organization that I represented everything negative they imagined about the company that was colonizing them. How did this demonstrate to my bosses that I would be useful to the company if given greater authority?

Showing a Broader Awareness of My Boss's Problems
Something I never asked myself at the time was what my boss had to deal with that went beyond the scope of my job. In other words, what would I have to know in addition to my present job if I were to be ready to do his? To begin with, my boss had to manage two other development teams, a sales force and several staff specialists. His world was broader than mine. If a decision was being considered that might negatively affect my project, did I simply do my best to protect my project or did I attempt to see the big picture and to fit my project into the broader needs of the company?

Still more broadly, my boss had to make decisions that were outside of the area where I worked. He had to deal much more with budgets and finances. He had to consider marketing issues. He participated in discussions about the changing company structure and his group's configuration. He had, especially, a much greater need to be able to align groups of people with differing views and to appease Sergeant Majors like myself who were likely to be angry or sullen if we did not get what we wanted.

As I look back, I can see that my efforts were almost entirely focused on the small part of my boss's work life that constituted my project. I treated the rest of his work life as a distraction or a threat to my success. This was not necessary. I could have attempted to better understand where I fit into his bigger picture. I could have learned from him about the job into which I wished to be promoted and, at the same time, I could have made him aware of my interest and abilities. One way to do this would have been to approach discussions with an attitude of "how can we find the best overall solution?" and not "this is what my team needs".

Stand Out as Somebody Who Fits In
Yes, I know this statement contradicts itself. It's an example of the more complex thinking that a Sergeant Major wishing to advance has to practice. Essentially, one has to stop thinking about perfection and think more about balance between contradictory factors. A Sergeant Major probably doesn't need to be told to stand out. I didn't. Fitting in is another story. Think of the ideal business suit. It isn't one that makes an impression; it's one that does not. The role of

a good outfit is to send subliminal signals of competency, neatness, appropriateness. The business suit that gets noticed has failed to do its job. That applies to us also.

How did I stand out? On the positive side, I made sure I was on schedule with a product that performed to specs. That was a good thing. I sent regular memos to the field sales and service people about the development of the product. That was good too. But in order to be noticed above the other memos (and I was) I did things that were not necessarily businesslike. My memo format (these were the ancient days before email) used a picture of the wizard Gandalf from the *Lord of the Rings* books. Realizing that the acronym of my product group (LPG) was also the name of a natural gas, I chose the inappropriate byline "passin' gas" for these memos.

Sometimes I used these memos to respond to criticisms from senior executives in a manner that amounted to putting them down in public. I may have been correct about the technical features in question, but that's irrelevant. I was playing the game for my own advantage, not that of my company. I was being noticed along with the product, but I was noticed for diverging from the culture, not for fitting into it.

Learn to Deal with Ambiguity
Sergeant Majors tend not to like ambiguity. Things are right or wrong, good or bad. Managers, however, live in a world of ambiguity. There is never enough good information to support decisions and what information exists is contradictory. Any solution creates new problems. Any course of action has negative as well as positive outcomes. Much is uncertain and unexpected. A Sergeant Major's desire for clarity and maximization of the good can work out very well for an individual project—it did for mine. It cannot work out well for a manager. To a great extent, the way I was acting as a project leader demonstrated that I should not be made a manager because I had attitudes and values that would torpedo me in that role.

Seek Mentoring Broadly
How was I to have known that by succeeding at my task I was demonstrating my lack of readiness for more authority? There

was nothing in my background to have warned me. My best resource would have been people already in the positions I want. The best medium for learning from them would have been informal conversation. This would have meant having more friendly relationships with those up the ladder. Why didn't I do this? There were several reasons.

For one thing, like many Sergeant Majors, I tended to identify with those who had less authority in the organization against those who had more. I am also a bit introverted, preferring a quiet lunch hour to a conversation, an evening at home to drinks with people from work. I was unaware that any of that activity was career related. I had not read this book, so I didn't know I was a Sergeant Major; I thought I was an executive in the making!

In retrospect, there is no doubt in my mind that more socializing at work and after work would have been the best way (1) to learn what I needed to know, (2) to learn to be better at those things (3) to demonstrate to those who make the decisions that I have the skills required in a position of more authority and (4) to build friendly relationships so that those who can promote me are more likely to think it is a good idea to do so.

In *The Soul of a New Machine*, Tracy Kidder tells the fascinating story of a group of Sergeant Majors who built a new computer for Data General around 1980. After surmounting impossible odds, these extremists produce the new machine successfully and it does well in the marketplace—far better than they do in their careers. Practically without exception, the Sergeant Majors responsible are reassigned to other impossible projects, resign to deal with their burnout or otherwise walk away from the table with little to show for their efforts except their salary checks. If you want to slay dragons against impossible odds, that's your prerogative. Just don't expect to be promoted for it.

Summing Up

What is happening to you isn't random and you aren't alone. If you're a Sergeant Major, you have millions of comrades-in-arms. You have value to your employer because you're competent and diligent, but you are up against a career glass ceiling because you have been working only on your job, not on your career. This is understandable; until now, you thought they were one and the same. Hopefully, you have also learned that you don't yet deserve to get ahead until you learn some new work skills. Don't worry; you can do this if you want to and we'll talk about how. First, though, let's look at how a Sergeant Major becomes a Sergeant Major.

CHAPTER 3:
WHERE DO SERGEANT MAJORS COME FROM?

✐

There are good reasons you became a Sergeant Major. It isn't a character defect that got you here. On the contrary, you probably have many fine qualities of character that are simply trapped in a dead-end situation. You aren't here because you're a slow learner. Indeed, you may be here because when bad advice was being handed out, it was your bad luck to be the most avid learner in the group. You got here largely as a result of good faith, good efforts and bad role models.

Of course, it is still your responsibility to decide what you will do about being a Sergeant Major. Understanding how you got here will not be useful if it just gives you somebody or something to blame. If you are interested in changing your situation, knowing how you got here can be a valuable part of learning how to have better choices about where to go from here. In this chapter, we will consider a number of common sources of "Sergeant Majordom".

Learning the Rules

There Are Two Rule Books (and You're Playing by the Wrong One)
Have you ever felt as though you were playing the game by the wrong rulebook? You probably are. More than twenty years ago,

Richard Ritti first published *The Ropes to Skip and the Ropes to Know*. Still in print and in its 7th edition, the enduring popularity of this book suggests that there is more to "knowing the ropes" than just following the rules. In any social group, your organization included, there are stated rules that must be followed. Of course you know that. But there are also rules that exist only on paper, which nobody follows. In addition, there are also rules that are not written down, but which you must follow. To frost the cake, people will usually not tell you which rules are which. Which ropes should you skip and which should you know? Learning this is a lifelong process. When I was a professor of Organizational Behavior I posted a greeting card on my office door that read, "Life is the only game where the purpose of the game is to learn the rules."

How do we learn these rules? There is no single place. We learn them from family, in school, at church, on the bus…everywhere. We are all exposed to a mixture of good and bad advice, but some of us receive more bad advice than others. It might be better to call what we have learned "limiting beliefs" rather than bad advice. That's because most of what we picked up was valid or useful in the context where we encountered it, but as we have taken this information into life without understanding the background that produced it, these beliefs limit rather than help us. Let's review some of the places we learned beliefs and attitudes that now limit us.

Limiting Beliefs in Early Life

Family
Families differ tremendously, but if you had come from one that gave you good role models for getting on in organizational life, you probably wouldn't be a Sergeant Major. What you learned wasn't necessarily wrong as much as it was right for a situation other than the one you now find yourself in. For instance, perhaps you grew up hearing, "the Lord helps those who help themselves" or "anything that's worth doing is worth doing well." From this, you learned that if you want something, work for it. That's a good lesson. What nobody added to that platitude, though was "– up to a point". Not everything worth doing is worth doing well, but you weren't told what is and is not worth the effort.

To a large extent, we were given answers rather a means for finding answers. Often, that is because what was passed on to us has become separated from the problems that produced the lesson. A friend of mine once told me of being taught by her mother to cut a roast in half before cooking it. After doing this for years, it occurred to her to ask why it had to be cut. Her mother said she didn't know; that's the way Grandma taught her. So my friend went to her grandmother and asked why she cut the roast in half. She was told, "Well, when I first started cooking roasts, I didn't have a pan large enough for it and we couldn't afford another one, so I would cut it in half to make it fit." In other words, for two generations the family had cut roasts in half to solve a problem that no longer existed.

When we learn that "God helps those who help themselves," "too many cooks spoil the broth", or "it's not what you know; it's who you know," we are being given answers cut off from the problems to which they are answers, but we take them on board and, by the time we are old enough to question them, they have become part of our taken-for-granted common sense.

Early Schooling
I once wrote that today's student who seems to have learned nothing in school, "has still learned to appear at a scheduled time, to sit in rows and columns of desks...not to raise questions...to do the task at hand without questioning its relevance." Alvin Toffler has called this the "covert curriculum", the things we absorb from our learning environment. For instance, in school, I learned that people are often quality-ranked by grades. The student who got 93 was measurably better than the student who got 88. The pecking order in class was clear and neat.

Of course, I was unlikely to question whether this was really the natural order of things because, as an excellent student, grade ranking made me one of the kids who was rewarded, applauded and held up to others as a role model. The limiting belief that came from this experience was my expectation that this model would also apply to organizational life. I thought that if my personnel file—my "grades"—showed me to be an A- employee that I would be rewarded proportionately more than the B+ employee. In retrospect, I could have learned more about organizational life by studying the playground at lunchtime.

In the school yard, I was lucky if being at the top of my class got me no attention at all because attention came in the form of teasing or bullying. Who has status in the schoolyard? It's a good deal more complex than a grade ranking. There are the leaders in games or sports. There is the class clown. There are those who offer the "wisdom" of their worldly experiences (even if they're making it up). There are the tough kids. As one gets older, there are the gatekeepers of contraband; alcohol, drugs, condoms, prohibited magazines. There is a complex overlap and interplay between pockets of leadership, each with their pecking order. The social life of the playground is complicated, one might even say tribal. We will discuss the tribal organization in the next chapter.

So, what did you learn from class instruction in school? We tend to pick up a simplified and polished view of the world. Those who succeed in life are those who deserve it. Bad things happen to bad people. The police protect good people. Government is here to help and authorities are all wise and benevolent. As we got older, did our ideas mature or are there bits and pieces of these simplistic notions still guiding our actions? You say you've dropped those ideas as you've gotten more cynical? That's not a defense. A cynic is a disappointed idealist. Developing mature attitudes is a different thing from having grown cynical.

Church

I do not criticize anybody's spiritual beliefs, but within every religion a wide variety of ideas are promoted by different clergy and a still wider variety are picked up by practitioners. For instance, if I am unhappy at work, it may reinforce my belief that I will suffer for my sins. If my life isn't turning out the way I hope, I may see it as evidence that if we accept humiliation in this world, we will be rewarded in the next. If I believe God is watching me and judging me, this belief may influence my general attitude toward the omniscience and fairness of authority figures.

None of this necessarily has to do with spirituality. It is about the leap we take when we move from the ether of our spiritual belief to the concrete realities of day to day life. The nature of God is not at issue. What needs to be examined is the nature of our attitudes as a result of our belief about God. The challenge for us is to notice where what was once religious dogma has become work habit, a way of looking at the world, a limiting belief.

Culture
People from different cultures have widely differing beliefs about what one can expect from life. Between the U.S. and England, to take two relatively similar cultures, there is little difference in the actual amount of social mobility in society, but a good deal of difference in the degree of mobility people believe to exist. In both countries, a Richard Branson or a Bill Gates can advance their fortunes dramatically. In both countries, too, the average person lives and dies in roughly the same economic circumstances in which they were born. Despite the evidence, Americans tend to believe that people are whatever they make of themselves, while the British tend to smile at what they see as American naiveté.

I once attended a presentation by a British theater company manager in which he commented that he had always considered it curious that the American Declaration of Independence should consider "pursuit of happiness" so achievable and so important as to declare it a fundamental human right. As an American, I was shocked. It had never occurred to me that anyone might question that "life, liberty and the pursuit of happiness" are anything but what the Declaration of Independence states them to be—self-evident. If there is a discrepancy between what I am experiencing in my career and what I expect, I might reflect a bit on the relationship between what I have been taught about advancing in the world and what I have learned about how the world works.

Limiting Beliefs in Our Careers
Early influences are not the only sources of limiting beliefs. As we proceed in life we are constantly exposed to new information that is often questionable and seldom subject to validation. These influences can also be understood in terms of the two rulebooks. If all we know is what is in the rulebook that is open to us, we will

have a distorted and potentially dangerous picture of how things operate in the world.

Blue-to-White Collar "Immigrants"

I lived for a number of years as an American in New Zealand. I know first hand what it means to be an immigrant to another country. It is disorienting because things mean differently to people from another culture. In the 1970s and 80s, I "emigrated" from blue collar work to white collar country. It was equally disorienting. Just as I will always be an American to New Zealanders, I will always have a bit of blue in my collar. This has effected my beliefs in many ways:

My first challenge was to learn the social graces of professional life. This began in college. I had to learn to speak and think differently in order to fit in. The process continued for years. Early in my professional life I would make jokes or observations about society that were seen as normal conversation in the working class community I came from, but which marked me as inappropriate in the white collar world. Some of these changes were fairly obvious, like using fewer of what George Carlin called the "seven words you can't say on television". Others were more subtle, like knowing how to speak about the columnist from the New York Times instead of the local tabloid.

This background has also marked how I look at organizational members. This became clearer to me when I left software development to become a management professor. As I have written elsewhere, the management disciplines formed as a network of relationships between professionals seeking the approval of senior executives. As a result, management texts talk to those executives about organizational problems as the execs see them. Not surprisingly, much of the management literature reflects the idea that senior management is the solution and individual contributors are the problem. It is also not surprising that, as an ex-blue collar worker, I tend to look through the other end of the telescope. To me, it seems pretty odd to suggest that the people with the least power in organizations have the power to be the biggest problem. I tend to notice where management fails to support the employee more than where the employee is deficient. Whether I am right or wrong, this limits me, both in getting on with my peers and in gaining the approval of those senior people whose view of me governs my advancement.

Blue collar people also have a different orientation to conflict. Where I grew up, a man was respected if he "didn't take any shit." This meant confronting people when one disagreed. It may have meant settling the matter with fists. If the conflict was verbal, it was still combative. The idea was to crush one's opponent. To the extent that I have any of this orientation left in my Sergeant Major behavior, it is limiting. In the professional world, the appropriate way to deal with conflict is to be polite in face-to-face exchange, to express differences indirectly, to negotiate, possibly to manipulate behind the scenes—but not to confront and challenge. When I was growing up, we had an entire vocabulary for people who deal with conflict indirectly and it was all unflattering. Now, I have to learn to be one. It's no small challenge.

"Secondary Ignorance"

I learned this wonderful term from a nurse who was telling me that some of the doctors she worked with suffered from it. Seeing the confusion on my face, she explained, "They don't know what they don't know". When I was a child, I believed what authority figures told me. My adult suspicion began when I started to see holes in their stories about Santa Claus, the Easter Bunny and the Tooth Fairy. Today, I know that advice from authorities has to be taken carefully.

As I have come to take advice more critically, I have noticed a paradoxical rule: On any issue, Those who are the least informed tend to be those who are the most certain and the most vocal. The *Dao De Ching* advises that "the farther you go; the less you will know." That has been my experience. Role models who teach that the truth is obvious, that anyone who disagrees is stupid or bad, do two disservices. The first is to teach you to apply simple solutions to complex problems. This is almost always inappropriate and less effective than listening, learning, negotiating and building shared agreement. But in addition, they may have been wrong to begin with! I grew up "knowing" that inter-racial dating was wrong, that smoking was cool and that my Protestant friends would all go to Hell. These were all limiting beliefs caused by sharing the secondary ignorance of others.

Film and TV
Have you ever watched the young hotshots sucking up to Donald Trump on *The Apprentice*? It might make good television, but it's a bad way to learn how to get on in an organization. I don't know if Trump runs his company this way, but if he does, it's a very unusual company. I'm not denying that there's competition and backbiting everywhere, or that there are winners and losers. The game is just played in a more subtle way. If you want to try to get ahead using what you saw on reality TV, you can count on getting "voted off the island".

Another genre is the "offices suck" theme we find in movies like *Office Space* and *Swimming with Sharks*, or *The Office* on TV. Sometimes these shows are brilliant sendups of office toxicity (I particularly love Jennifer Anniston's conversation with her boss about her "flair" in *Office Space*), but we need to be careful not to pick up their attitude. It's your right to think your workplace is soul destroying, but as long as you do, expect to be marginal there. The people who get authority are those who can believe something positive about the place.

Workplace (Mis)Information
If you're a Sergeant Major, you already know that a large portion of your workplace information is speculative. Is your new technical specialist sleeping with your boss? Did the head of western sales say that your product line is a waste of space in the sales catalog? What does your boss really think about you relative to the three other team leaders who answer to her? Who believed your memo explaining that the delays you are experiencing are beyond your control? In business, we always have too little information. Some of it is inaccurate and we don't usually know which part. This makes us susceptible to misinformation.

For instance, I was once in a situation where my boss convinced me that he was supporting me, but that his good efforts were being stonewalled by his boss. It took me more than a year to learn that my boss was the problem and his boss was my solution. By that time, I had lost a year pushing against a brick wall instead of making progress. Worse, I had shown my negative feelings to my boss's boss and had to do damage control before I could start to make progress in that relationship.

We also need to manage outgoing information so that we are not misunderstood. I once sent a letter to my former bosses in another division stating that we needed to take steps to keep my product from becoming a "tin-plated" version of the parent company's analogous product. The memo was shown to my current boss, and he was furious with me, both for going around him to people in another division and for calling his product tin plated. That I had been trying to act proactively to keep his product from being seen as second rate didn't matter. What hurt me was the fact that I had managed information poorly and, as a result, I was seen by my boss as undermining him.

Management Education

Maybe you have a degree in management? There is a lot one can learn from business study, but it is also a good place to pick up limiting beliefs. Most of the mistakes I made as a Sergeant Major were made *after* completing my MBA! One limiting belief that has been criticized by leading management educators such as Henry Mintzberg is the impression one can get from business school that reality is controlled from a spreadsheet. Of the twelve MBA courses I took while pursuing my degree, eleven involved trying to come up with a brilliant solution to a problem by crunching numbers. Only one taught me about the messiness of interpersonal behavior—and that one, Introductory Organizational Behavior, only introduced useful topics. It neither took us very far nor suggested how much farther an effective manager would have to go.

As I noted above, management study is also shaped by its history. Our management knowledge has developed primarily to help major employers get large numbers of unwilling employees to do routine factory work. The central problem was the unwilling employee. This probably has little to do with your work as a Sergeant

Major. It is more likely that everyone you work with wants to do the job as they see it, but everyone is heading in a somewhat different direction toward divergent goals. Lessons we learned helping Ford effectively build the Model A at River Rouge can be a barrier to your effectiveness more easily than they can help.

Gender
Certain demographic characteristics can increase or decrease the likelihood of our becoming Sergeant Majors by influencing the experience we have as we go through life. Gender is one of these. The role of gender will be different across cultures and at different times, but the beliefs we learn in becoming a man or a woman are powerful influences on our careers.

In the U.S., for instance, as in many countries, there has been a huge increase of women in professional positions in the last two generations. On the one hand, sexism has diminished slowly, so that there are innumerable ways one can more easily be seen as a leader if one is a man. Coupled to this, women pioneers in professional roles are likely to have gotten the partial truth of "to get ahead, work hard" referred to above. Both of these factors push in the same direction—toward giving the successful project leader another, and more impossible, project.

On the whole, these women have shown a greater awareness than men of the importance of "invisible work", work that contributes to the success of the organization, but that disappears from evaluation processes. Helping others, coordinating between people who need to collaborate, brokering peace where there are disagreements, looking after the booking of meetings, travel and catering—all of these are examples of invisible work and, on the whole, women have shown a much greater awareness of their importance than men. This too can contribute to one becoming a Sergeant Major. As I noted in chapter two, you can't be recognized for work nobody knows about.

On the other hand, if we are the type of men who learned limiting beliefs about settling differences through combat, we are likely to find the women we work with more skilled at negotiating difficulties. We might well learn from them how to better get on by working diplomatically instead of aggressively. But be careful. I have been saying women and men "in general". There is huge variation among individual women and among individual men. Gender is a powerful influence, but it is not destiny.

Peer Groups

Have you ever worked in a job where you came home dirty? I did from age twelve to twenty six. One common way laborers assert the value of their occupations is to talk, joke and think in ways suggesting that to get dirty at work is ennobling; that wearing dress clothes and carrying a laptop is for sissies. With skilled workers, these differences may be more subtle, but they are likely to be there. Not so long ago I consulted with a biotech company in which the culture valued practicing scientists. To leave the "real" work and go into management had low esteem.

As you negotiate your career, make sure these differing group norms don't cause you to be locked into unproductive limiting beliefs. You are unlikely to succeed in management (if you even get there in the first place) if your attitude is that the engineers do the real work. Here comes that nasty word again: "balance". You need to learn to be an effective boundary spanner if you are going to have upward mobility and credibility. Within the sales group, you need to be seen as valuing sales. Within the management group, you need to show you value management. Sometimes, each group will look at the other as the source of all their problems. That makes the balancing act more difficult, but no less necessary.

Psychological Limiting Beliefs

In addition to cultural factors and career experiences, a wide variety of events in our psychological histories can have an influence on "Sergeant Majordom". This point will be inapplicable to many readers, but it applies to enough of us to be worth mentioning.

Recovery from Psychological Trauma

Many people come from traumatic family backgrounds characterized by poverty, instability, substance abuse, physical or sexual violence. People tend to react to these terrible circumstances in one of several fairly predictable ways. In the popular literature on this subject there are about a half-dozen archetypes, each of which represents a common response to an abusive past. I would like to focus on three: the Hero, the Placator and the Lost One.

The Hero is one who tries to overcome the past by doing everything right. Sometimes Heroes have extraordinary achievements because they are more driven than those around them. Heroes may also find themselves on the Sergeant Major plateau because of the limiting beliefs they still hold. After all, given their past, they have had questionable role models. No matter how driven they are, if they drive down a blind alley, they will stop moving forward.

The Placator is like a good middle child, good at defusing conflict, finding common ground, soothing hurt feelings. You can see the advantages a Placator might have in helping a group of people get to a goal, but this can be a two-edged sword. Given that these qualities were shaped by trauma, a Placator may need, to suppress conflict. Some conflict is healthy and constructive. A work group led by a Placator may be handicapped by a limited ability to process differences of opinions and to discuss divergent ideas.

A Lost One has learned not to be a target for those with more power by being invisible. One way to do this is to disappear into work. A Lost One may be a valuable individual contributor. He finally got the trade show display together at four in the morning. She was found asleep at her desk after having worked forty-two hours straight before the new product release. They leafleted as many houses in the last election as any other three volunteer teams for Senator X. On the down side, Lost Ones can disrupt a team by outdistancing the others or setting a bad work/life balance example. With skills that are so task centered, they may be lacking in the interpersonal skills needed to negotiate with other groups in the company, with suppliers, contractors and customers. While a Lost One is likely to be a poor manager, many Lost Ones are such high-performing individual contributors that they are promoted—to Sergeant Major.

If you have a history with substance abuse and recovery, it would also not be surprising if you have qualities of the Hero or Lost

One. This book is not about family psychology. If any of these are relevant to your life, I suggest you look at some of the resources on the reading list I have provided. Counseling can also be useful. At the moment, I would just suggest you look at your background and ask yourself honestly where the beliefs you have developed as a consequence of this history are being useful to you and where they are limiting.

If you are working on any issues for which there is a 12-Step group (there are now more than a hundred kinds), this can be a useful tool for looking at Sergeant Major behavior. The central messages of 12-Step programs revolve around learning to fit in rather than to stand apart, to get along by going along, to become more flexible and less brittle, to become less self centered—all without losing your integrity. These messages are so consistent with what we need to hear as Sergeant Majors that those of us without 12-Step issues might envy those who have this free self-help network available to them!

Co-dependency

"Give that problem to Pat. She'll take care of it." Most organizations have one or more Pats. Are you one? Up to a point, being a person who gets things done is a good thing, but past a certain point the need to respond to any need of the organization becomes destructive to you—and eventually perhaps even to the organization. In the psychological literature, this is discussed as co-dependency. Although co-dependency is usually treated as a psychological problem, I prefer the way it is described by Anne Wilson Schaef—as an attempt to be healthy within an unhealthy system. The classic illustration of co-dependency is the spouse of an alcoholic whose dependability and nurturing enable the alcoholic to continue being undependable and irresponsible. As always, the key point at issue is balance. Up to a point, responsibility is, of course, desirable. Past a certain point, it is destructive to the responsible individual.

I recently spoke to a friend who is the chief financial officer for a troubled organization. She was complaining that she had not had the time to grieve the recent death of her spouse because she was working too hard to save the organization. After all, she explained, two hundred people's jobs depended on her efforts. Perhaps she is right. The question is: at what point does one put one's own legitimate needs over the demands of the organization? Where is the balance point and how does one know when one has crossed it? Considering the dynamics of co-dependency, especially as they are discussed by Schaef in *Co-Dependence: Misunderstood, Mistreated*, can help us better identify that line.

"Giftedness"

Do you know your I.Q.? Psychologists commonly refer to people with an I.Q. over 130 (2.5% of the population) as "gifted". Not all Sergeant Majors are gifted, but gifted people are especially likely to become Sergeant Majors. High-IQ people tend to deal with the world around them differently from others, to misunderstand others and to be misunderstood in return. It is not true that giftedness is a "gift" (which is why most gifted people dislike the term). It is a potential. In order to realize that potential, the gifted person must learn to build a bridge between their reality and the mainstream world. If you think this may apply to you, there is excellent online material available. Try searching "gifted adult." Two particularly good resources are the web sites of Lynn Azpeitia and Stephanie Tolan.

Personality

Strictly speaking, personality is not a limiting belief, but it is useful to consider while you are looking at limiting beliefs. Not so long ago, I took a personality test for a sales job. It asked me to agree/disagree on items like, "I like most people I meet" and "I believe most people are basically honest." In management, as in sales, two personality qualities stand out so prominently as to be almost entry requirements: optimism and extroversion.

I mean optimism in a very broad sense. It is not just belief that you will be successful, but belief that the people you meet are generally well intentioned and competent and that your organization is basically effective and worth working for. Here's a quick Sergeant Major test. Take a moment to look at the items on www.Successories.com. You have probably seen them around many offices. Now check out www.Despair.com, a parody of the Successories items. Which do you prefer? Of course you do! I think the parody items are brilliant. I desperately want to display them in my office. Why don't I? Because cynics may be appreciated and gallows humor may draw an appreciative audience. But the promotion is going to go to the person who can display the Successories poster with a straight face.

Extroversion is about the degree to which a person enjoys interacting with others. I like the way it is defined by the Myers-Briggs personality test. According to that model, an extrovert is somebody who gains energy from personal interaction. An introvert is somebody for whom personal interaction has an emotional cost. Before interacting, an introvert will weigh whether the anticipated value of the interaction will outweigh the cost. I'm somewhat introverted. When I fly, I prefer that the person next to me not bother me with meaningless chitchat because I'm never going to see them again anyway. An extrovert would chat because the chat is its own reward.

Many Sergeant Majors are introverted cynics, but whether we like it or not, it's an optimistic extrovert's world. This isn't coincidental. Like sales, managing relies primarily on dealing effectively with people and an extroverted optimist has a dual advantage in that regard. Within limits, you can change your personality. This is what every major self help book in history has advocated, "The power of positive thinking." To the extent that you can't or don't want to change, this is still good to be aware of because you have to ask yourself what the best option is for a person with your skills and personality. You might make a great team leader. You might be suited for self employment. But it may not be a good investment of your energy to try to advance in an organization when your personality is saying, "I am in opposition to the group I am trying to join."

Taking Control of Your Limiting Beliefs

Here is an exercise to help you gain control of your limiting beliefs:

BECOMING AWARE OF YOUR LIMITING BELIEFS

1. First, make a numbered list of the factors that have contributed to your present limiting beliefs. The bullet points in this chapter are a good starting point, but feel free to add or delete items.
2. Keep this list handy. Every time you encounter a problem at work or are feeling down about your job/career, make a 15 minute appointment with yourself to reflect on this list.
3. For 15 minutes, do not let yourself be disturbed or distracted. Using a notebook or a computer, set aside a page for this problem. At the top of the page, write a brief summary of the problem in enough detail that you can come back to it later and know what was happening.
4. Under the description, make a list of all the limiting beliefs you can think of (yours, not those of others!) that have contributed to causing this problem, to aggravating it or to preventing it from being solved. Number each entry on the list with the number of the source of that belief. For example, "2. I was upset about not getting a raise because I thought it was like getting a grade in school."
5. Initially, it may be hard to see any limiting beliefs at all. Here's a hint. *Assume the problem is your fault.* This may not be true, but if you start here, you will probably see ways you could have minimized or avoided the problem. Remember, having a good excuse for being in trouble is a child's defense. An adult's responsibility is to avoid it or to fix it.
6. Once a week, set aside time to go over your entire set of notes and think about how your limiting beliefs are connected to the way you work. As you become more aware of this connection, you can start to make more conscious decisions about what beliefs you want to take to work with you.

There is a widely repeated simple aphorism that I believe originates with Rheinhold Neibuhr:

> Grant me the patience to accept the things I cannot change.
> The courage to change the things I can
> And the wisdom to know the difference.

The power of this aphorism lies in the fact that it directs us to focus our energies on the things we can change rather than squandering them on things that are beyond our reach. As Sergeant Majors, we are likely to have a well-developed blueprint for determining how the universe should be run. The problem is that the universe never consults us. It may be true that your V.P of marketing really doesn't understand the value of your product's features. Your boss may really be an idiot. Customers may indeed be expressing an ignorant preference for the inferior product. The question you have to ask yourself is, "What can I do about this?" Where you can make a constructive contribution, go for it. Where the problem is beyond your control, it isn't a problem; it's a fact of your life.

One of the things you do have considerable power to change is your understanding of the rules that govern your work life. Start thinking differently about these rules. Don't resort to "common sense", which is nothing more than your accumulated limiting beliefs. Make studying the rules part of your job description.

Summing Up

When I was ten years old, part of the misinformation in my peer group included the occasional story about somebody we knew seeing a book containing the "facts of life" open in the parish rectory. We imagined this as more or less a page of bullet points. Now that I know more about sexuality, I know that "the facts of life" is a metaphor, shorthand for something very complex, something that means different things to different people. There can be no simple list of these "facts". The same is true of organizational rules. Stop confusing them with the policies in human resources and the memos you receive. Those are a legitimate part of the rules, but they are only a part (Even then, part of them should be ignored, but which part?!).

I hope this chapter has started you thinking about three key points:

1. One of the main obstacles to your career satisfaction is the unproductive way you frame the problems you encounter. This occurs because of limiting beliefs which you have picked up in life and which are part of your taken-for-granted common sense.

2. You are **not** responsible for having these limiting beliefs. Mostly they came from experiences that were beyond your control, from taking unhelpful advice from people you had reason to trust or from extending useful advice into a context where it ceased to be useful

3. You **are** responsible for what you do with these limiting beliefs.

Learning the unwritten rules is a lifetime's work. You will never completely master them. The rules change over time and some change when you change companies. I once worked for a company where one of the unwritten rules of getting ahead in management involved marijuana, cocaine and trading Grateful Dead bootleg concert tapes. To make matters worse, this culture dominated only part of the company so one not only had to know the unstated rule, but the invisible boundary of the rule's domain! How do we become better at learning and working with such fluid and unstated rules? That is the central point of the next chapter.

CHAPTER 4:
THE TRIBAL ORGANIZATION

S ergeant majors tend to treat organizations the way sports players treat their game. There is a rule book and a referee to assign penalties when the rules are broken. There is a winner and a loser based on points. Those who play well according to the rules are valued more than those who don't. Work is like baseball; the .330 hitter is recognized as a slugger and the .190 hitter is just a slug.

This does explain part of organizational life, but just a part. Sometimes, your bosses will notice you doing well and you will get "points" for it. Sometimes your KPIs (key performance indicators) and performance review will accurately reflect your contributions. Sometimes, the highest quality project will be seen as the best by those who count. Sometimes people will give you the opportunity to demonstrate your distinct skills by solving a problem that others can't.

Sometimes.

And sometimes, you will work your butt off, but those who count won't notice. Sometimes, your team's minor failures will be held against it while the major successes are passed over. Sometimes you will be hurt because the bosses selected somebody they like for a key position, passing over the person with the best skills. The world is imperfect and only partially refereed. If you have been playing only by the rule book and you are waiting for the ref to blow the whistle and call the goal for your team, there is something you need to know:

Organizations are tribal.

A tribe is a group of people held together, not by rules, but by *relationships*. In a modern work organization, the tribal organization co-exists with the organization that operates from explicit rules and procedures. Let's call the organization of rules the bureaucratic organization. You might say that the tribal organization constitutes the context within which the organization of rules is embedded. It should not be surprising that the bureaucratic organization is a veneer on the deeper, tribal relationships. After all, we have operated bureaucratic organizations for only a couple of centuries. We have organized tribally since the beginning of time.

There Are Two Organizations in Every Organization

The Bureaucratic Organization
We tend to use the word "bureaucracy" only to denote organizational situations that are buried in red tape. That is not what I mean. The term comes to us from the German sociologist, Max Weber, who used the term "bureaucracy" to describe a form of organizing that only came to prominence in the nineteenth century. In the bureaucratic organization, individual authority is subordinated to rules. Ideally, an office holder enforces the rules applicable to that office rather than governing based on personal whim. When one person is replaced by another, there should be no change because both are held to the same set of rules. Differences of individual preference do not enter into things. This ideal is never perfectly achieved, of course, but it is the principal on which things are organized.

The idea of bureaucracy is wrapped up with another notion, "meritocracy." If the rules determine what happens and the rules are enforced appropriately, those who perform better receive proportionately better evaluations and rewards. Merit is rewarded fairly. I don't have to tell you that the perfect meritocracy doesn't exist. You know that. You may, however, still be under the impression that the perfect meritocracy should exist. When you see preference, recognition or authority being distributed on any principle other than bureaucratic merit, do you consider this a failing of the system? Do you complain bitterly? Does it seem unfair? Perhaps it is, but have you considered the possibility that a principle completely different from bureaucracy or merit is controlling what happens?

The Tribal Organization

The tribal metaphor may have you thinking of hunter-gatherer societies, people in loincloths heading out with spears to kill dinner. That's appropriate enough, but we don't have to reach so far to find organizations that are almost entirely tribal. Street gangs are tribal; so is organized crime and prison life. Illegal organizations are particularly excellent illustrations of tribal organizations because they don't have recourse to the law and have reasons to not keep bureaucratic records. Voluntary organizations are highly tribal, whether we are talking about an outlaw motorcycle gang or the local country club. If you have never been a Mafioso or served time in San Quentin, there is another tribal organization I know you participated in—childhood.

If you are a good Sergeant Major, the odds are high that you were more successful negotiating the well-structured life of the classroom than the turbulent world of the playground. In class, everyone played by the rules and the teacher was a diligent referee. The rules for succeeding were clear and you were good at them. The playground was both a murkier and a more violent world. There were different groups and each had different rules for leadership and recognition. The jocks had one society. The stoners had another. The tough kids had yet another. One thing all the groups had in common, though, was ostracizing and punishing those who didn't fit in. Remember what a complicated dance it was not to be stigmatized as one of the kids who was cruelly picked on?

Tribal behavior in the office is less overtly cruel and violent. You probably don't have to worry about having your head stuck in a toilet while you get a "flushie" and they're unlikely to work perversions of your name into rude chants like, "Roy, toy, the hot dog boy". But the office tribe is still held together by the same set of rules that organized the playground. If you want to see the tribal way of treating organizational outsiders, rent a movie like *North Country, Men of Honor,* or the first *Prime Suspect* mini-series. In a work organization, the bureaucratic rules that ordered the classroom are best thought of as a thin network of formal procedures laid over a solidly tribal base.

The Tribal "Rulebook"

A mistake you may have made—that I certainly made—is to think that the classroom is the important reality to negotiate and the playground is, well, just for play. That's backwards. If you can negotiate the playground, you can negotiate life. But, if you were good at negotiating the playground, I'm guessing you wouldn't be a Sergeant Major. The rules of the tribe constitute the second "rulebook" I mentioned earlier. This is the hidden rulebook you may have overlooked or misinterpreted. Let's look at some of the unwritten rules that hold tribes together:

THE TRIBAL ORGANIZATION

1. The rules are implicit; you learn them by doing them.
2. The tribe is composed of *relationships*.
3. Relationships are based on similarity.
4. Membership and power are linked to the person, not the role.
5. Allegiance to the tribe is more important than skill or brilliance.
6. Membership is informal, undocumented and unbounded.
7. Allies and opponents are difficult to distinguish from each other.

---

1. The Rules Are Implicit; You Learn Them By Doing Them.

One reason I don't dance is that when people have tried to teach me they have tended to lead me onto a dance floor, then say something like, "Just do what you feel." When they say that, What I feel is that I'd be happier standing at the bar. I want somebody to give me the Arthur Murray version: left foot here…right over there… hand on your hip…turn this way. I want *explicit* rules.

The bureaucratic organization has explicit rules. If I am at my desk by 8.30 I am okay. If I arrive at 8.40, I am in violation of the rules. If I meet five of my six KPIs I am eligible for a merit raise. I like explicit rules. Unfortunately, much of my life is controlled by implicit rules. What are the implicit rules? The idea of "fitting in" covers a lot of it. You learn the implicit rules by observing what others are doing and doing it yourself. There is no rule book and there is usually little or no instruction. You just get on the dance floor and do it.

There is another reason I don't dance. When learning implicit rules, you have no choice but to go through a period of performing poorly until you learn to perform better. I could never bear the thought of being seen as dancing badly, so I didn't do it at all. That's only one place my prejudice against implicit rules has hurt me. Fraternity hazing rituals are an integral part of tribal life. Everybody in the tribe has to be the butt of the joke sometime. The challenge is to learn when, not to avoid it completely.

2. The Tribe Is Composed of *Relationships.*

According to Max Weber, the most radical new feature of the bureaucratic organization was the fact that authority and responsibility were attached to roles, not to individuals. Ideally, it should make no difference whether Brad or Brenda is the business development manager attached to your product group. When Brad is transferred and Brenda takes his place, you expect the business development manager to continue to link you to marketing and to clients the way it was done in Brad's day. That's because it's the role of the business development manager that you are connected to rather than the individual.

Of course, you know that Brenda will do the job a bit differently from Brad and you will have to establish a personal connection, but in the bureaucratic organization, you expect that the role will remain largely unchanged. Brad and Brenda are both expected to operate to policy, not to make it up as they go along. This expectation will be higher if you do not have a face-to-face relationship with your business development manager. If I am in Palo Alto and Brenda is in Amsterdam,

I am likely to expect that nothing will change when she becomes my business development manager except the e-mail address I use to communicate her. In the tribal organization, this is not so.

I was once told that I had been hired for a sales position with a metals distributor because I listed running as a recreational activity on my resume. The manager of that facility was a runner and he liked runners. That was a tribal relationship. As it turned out, I was pretty bad at selling metals and a couple of the guys who did it well would have had trouble running to the coffee machine. In the tribal organization, relationships are not necessarily about role-relevant qualities. I have worked in situations where playing golf with my peers and bosses, playing lunchtime chess—even snorting coke in hotel rooms --- were key elements of tribal relationships (For the record, I did none of these—especially the golf!).

Relationships are also based on what the group does not do or like. The metals job I just referred to required sales staff to work in the warehouse one day a year for inventory. We were told to dress for warehouse work, but weren't told what that dress was. Appropriate dress would have been something like old chinos and a sweater. I showed up wearing Western boots, jeans and a leather jacket, looking more like a real shop floor worker than an office guy who had been loaned out for one day. On seeing me, my boss made a good natured joke about not recognizing me, "I thought it was some hippie walking in." You can bet that wardrobe choice labeled me as an outsider to the office "tribe."

3. Relationships Are Based on Similarity.

In her landmark book, *Men and Women of the Corporation*, Rosabeth Moss Kanter described the way organizations recruit and promote new members as "homosocial reproduction." What she was suggesting is that we tend to see people who are like ourselves as being "better". If I am hiring an engineer, the fact that he went to the same school I did, knows several of my old professors, shares my interest in parasailing and has political opinions that resonate with mine has nothing at all to do with his ability to do the job. It is, however, likely to positively color my opinion about his ability. Conversely, if he is culturally very different from me, that can hurt him.

The more objective the job requirements are, the less important tribal considerations are. If I am hiring a Mercedes salesperson and Keisha has won the monthly sales contest for 17 of the last 24 months at the BMW showroom down the road, her record pretty much speaks for itself. In a job where 98% of hires last less than six months, she has pretty objective evidence that, if I hire her, both her family and mine will eat well. Now, if you are looking for advancement to a management position, how objective is the evidence for your case?

Not very.

It is hard to determine how well a manager is doing. The job involves doing a thousand things, many of which are not directly connected to outcomes. Conversely, outcomes may be determined by many things other than good or bad management. Because the evidence held by the bureaucratic organization gives me little help in determining how well a person is managing or how suitable they are for the role, much of the information I will necessarily rely on will be based on tribal relationships. The Sergeant Major who overlooks this overlooks most of the decision-making process.

If you are a member of my tribe and I presume you are competent, maybe your team's bad performance was because of the economic downturn, the recent restructuring, your investment in future performance, bad weather or gremlins. If you are not of good standing within my tribe, even your good performance could be explained away as resulting from a coincidental surge in residual customer demand, from good people carrying your bad performance, from good weather or blind good luck. I cannot know with much certainly what your efforts accomplished. I can know with much more certainty how much you are or are not like the people I consider to be effective.

In my experience as a manager or as a business owner, I have seldom been in a position where the information I needed for decision making was adequate. Having no alternative, even a good manager makes decisions based on the best, bad information available. What this means for you in your career is:

If I presume you are effective, I am unlikely to be proven wrong.

If I presume you are ineffective, I am unlikely to be proven wrong.

What I presume shapes "the facts" more than the facts "speak for themselves".

4. Membership and Power Are Linked to the Person, not the Role.

I once worked in an organization where roles were defined exceptionally poorly. If I had a problem with my computer, I didn't call the IT help desk because very little help was available there. I called Gerhard in IT because he could help me. Similarly, when my online teaching platform failed, I called Duncan, not WebCT service. When the projector wouldn't work in lecture, I called Ravi on his personal cell phone—I never even learned where his office was. And so it went through the entire work day. To those of us used to the bureaucratic organization, this is poor management, but for most of history, this was simply how people organized. The idea of a standardized role that is more or less the same no matter who is in it is a product of the nineteenth century.

The tribe precedes the nineteenth century by many millennia. In the tribe, it is not so much your job title, but your personal skills that matter. These may be work related if you are the project wizard who solves the problems everyone else can't, but it may be other skills: your connection to a key supplier or customer, your engagement to the boss's nephew, even the fact that everyone loves the parties you throw. Your position may be based on strength of character, as it is in gangs, as it was on the schoolyard.

The lesson to take from this is that you cannot look at your work life only in terms of roles. If you want to move from one role to another, you must look at where you stand in the tribal relationships that determine where you stand. Your work skill is relevant, but it is only a part of what matters. How you get along with people is also important, but that is not enough either. Get into the habit of asking where you stand in the tribe. Compare yourself to other tribe members. Ask yourself where they stand and why.

You have probably done this already, but not in a productive way. You noticed the tribal behavior, but dismissed it as inappropriate "schmoozing," "brown nosing," "ass kissing" or worse. Put on a new pair of glasses. These are glimpses of people engaging in important tribal relations. Try to understand what is happening in terms of cause and effect rather than judgment.

5. Allegiance to the Tribe Is More Important Than Skill or Brilliance.

One of the most important observations I have ever read about organizations is from *Experiences in Groups*, a pioneering book written by Wilfred Bion about the dynamics of people in groups. In it, Bion suggests that once a group forms, its most important role becomes the preservation of the group. This goes deeper than "turf" or organizational "empire building". It is a basic human behavior. Perhaps it has to do with our evolution as social animals, dependent on each other for survival, but for whatever reason, it is pervasive. Loyalty to the group is the fundamental principal of the tribal organization.

Maintaining the group may have deep psychological origins, but it is also related to group effectiveness. Even when I ran an organization with only a couple dozen employees, most things were done by groups of people, not by individuals. Each person could do their job effectively only if they knew how those on whom they depended would do theirs. The person who protects the group protects the organization. The person who diverges, even to be outstanding, is a threat to effectiveness. As organizations grow, they quickly come to have multiple tribal groups. Nobody, anywhere, can work for "the good of the organization." What would that be? We work for our own good or the good of our tribes. We usually think of our tribes as serving "the good of the organization"—but so do all the other tribes working for different goals.

We can better understand the importance of tribal allegiance if we look at how quickly organizational communication paths become unmanageable if they are not limited by rules or tribal norms. The chart below shows the number of communication pathways in organizations of different sizes. When I hire my first employee, there are only two paths; I can speak to you or you can speak to me. One more employee does not increase the number of pathways to three, but to six. As we grow, the number of communication pathways grows faster. Even in a relatively small organization of 100 people, there are already 9,900 communication possibilities!

Number of Employees	Communication Pathways
2	2
3	6
4	12
5	20
10	90
25	600
50	2450
100	9900

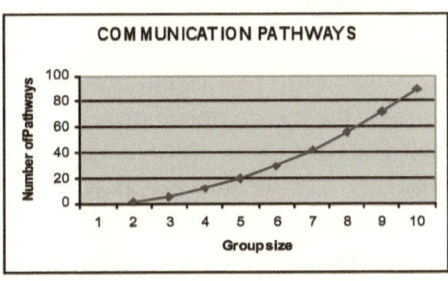

Bear in mind that in order to get work done, individuals depend on each other. Suppose that in an organization of one hundred people, six people need to communicate in order to successfully complete a task. That means there are six to twelve appropriate communication paths and well over 9,800 inappropriate ones. Without established procedures in place, the chance that the appropriate communication paths will not be buried by inappropriate paths is only about one percent! In an organization of any size, the chances are about zero. This tends to engender a very conservative attitude in those who are responsible for getting things done.

There are two ways to channel communication effectively. The bureaucratic way is through rules. The tribal way is through group loyalty. A factory is an example of an environment where the rules dominate. On the factory floor, the worker tribe is usually a problem management wishes to control. The result is a rigid, control-heavy organization that can only perform highly programmable tasks like auto assembly. The more an organization relies on worker discretion for innovation or flexibility, the less effective rules are and the more central tribal relationships become.

In this environment, the dependable star might hypothetically be more valuable than the loyal plodder, but stars tend to decide for themselves when to follow the rules and when to make their own. This means the plodder is usually a better choice because they can be counted on by the group. Remember Nathan from chapter two, the brilliant, likeable, industrious counter worker—who I fired?

6. Membership Is Informal, Undocumented, Unbounded and Dynamic.

These examples illustrate a quality common to tribal rules in general: *there is no documentary evidence that the rules exist at all.* That means there is no right to protest them. Worse still, you will often not even know when they are operating against you. When your boss and a couple other senior executives asked your peer on another team to go to the hockey game with them and you weren't asked, you didn't even know about it. If people tend to go around, rather than through, you on workplace business, you will have only the vaguest idea of what you are missing. As they say, there are three kinds of people: those in the loop; those out of the loop and those who don't know there is a loop. When you are out of the loop, you know it and can work on it. When you don't know there is a loop, you're helpless.

Because the rules that govern informal relationships can't be proven, there is no boundary to them. There is a limit to how bad a performance review I can give to somebody I dislike, but who does an excellent job in their role. On the other hand, if I don't like this person, there is a great deal of valuable, but informal, information I can withhold from her "accidentally". I can "forget" to circulate the new price sheets to her. I can make sure she's away on a day trip to Cleveland when the corporate management team visits and others have a chance to make a good impression and perhaps meet potential mentors. I can assign her the most impossible project and say it's because, "I know you are the best person for this challenge." Until I violate company policy or employment law, she is helpless to respond because I can deny that I am treating her any differently than the others. As long as I step between the threads of the bureaucratic net and rely on tribal relationships, my ability to hinder her is unbounded.

Tribal relationships are also dynamic; they change. In many workplaces, negative attitudes toward women and people of color which would have marked me as tribal insider a couple generations ago now mark me as an outsider. A corporate merger can result in a change of culture with resultant changes in what informal rules govern the formation of key relationships. Company growth has the same effect. An organization of 500 probably operates on different rules than it did when it was a single tribe of 30. Although these relationships tend to be durable, meaning that they are unlikely to change randomly or overnight, they also evolve. They are in constant flux.

7. Allies and Opponents Are Difficult to Distinguish from Each Other.

Another relevant lesson from the *Godfather* movies is Michael Corleone's advice to, "keep your friends close, but your enemies closer." It took me quite awhile to learn that when a manager tells me that I "don't suffer fools gladly," the stated message and the deeper meaning are quite different from each other. On the surface, the message sounds like a compliment, especially if delivered with a smile. What it means, though, is that I'm impatient and intolerant, a liability to the smooth functioning of the group. The good manager will not see me literally as the enemy, but will see me as somebody who needs to be watched and contained. The good manager knows that this is better done with a smile than with a cage.

Were that manager a Sergeant Major, the message might be easier to decode when he says to me: "What the hell is your problem? Is somebody off their meds today?" Then I'd know he disapproved. But, being more attuned to the tribal functioning of the organization, our managers realize that it is more effective to respond in a way that leaves us feeling part of the group. The insincere compliment keeps us close, but not necessarily as a friend. You have probably noticed managers keeping superficial appearances friendly while noting that some of those they are friendly to are people with whom they have difficulties. You probably called this acting two-faced or hypocritical. Try to look at this behavior another way. Appreciate how holding your friends close and your enemies closer helps to hold the tribal organization together by maximizing possibilities for cooperation and minimizing destructive conflict.

Effective Organizations Need Tribes

Tribalism isn't just a primitive holdover in the modern, bureaucratic organization. As people, being members of groups is deeply embedded in us. Groups have a powerful effect in motivating and demotivating us. When I was a teenager, I wore some incredibly uncomfortable and questionable looking clothing. Why? It labeled me as a member of the group I thought was cool.

Consider the extreme case of soldiers in combat. It is hard to imagine a human activity more unnatural than voluntarily going where people are trying to kill you and, in return, trying to kill perfect strangers. In fact, when in combat, a very high percentage of soldiers freeze up and do not fight. Much research has been done on why soldiers fight. under fire; bravery, patriotism, family, religion and duty don't explain as much as loyalty to the platoon, to the group one fights with. This is no less true in the office "cubicle farm" than in the foxhole.

The limitation of tribes is that, unlike the bureaucratic organization, they can't perform particularly complex activities. A warlord leading a mob has little chance against a modern, professional army. Modern organizations are composed of complex groups of tribes, coordinated by the bureaucratic organization. The bureaucratic overlay of procedures, role definitions, reporting relationships and strategic goals permits coordination of tribal efforts to achieve goals mere tribes or bureaucracies could never reach on their own. A tribal R&D group probably generated the technical insight that permitted the cell phone, but without the bureaucratic organization, the new technology could never have become an everyday consumer product. In the modern organization, tribalism and bureaucracy are inseparable.

A good Sergeant Major is likely to have encountered the tribal organization in two contradictory ways. On the one hand, many Sergeant Majors build effective teams. Competency, devotion to getting the job done well, caring about one's people and being willing to lead by example are all qualities common to Sergeant Majors. There is a high degree of tribalism in these qualities. Getting to the goal by building strong, positive group relationships is tribal. If there is a likely downside to the way a Sergeant Major is tribal, it is the possibility that setting the group competitively against other groups and harassing management on behalf of the group may have resulted in the group succeeding *against* the organization rather than with it.

Oddly, while we are frequently highly sensitive to these aspects of tribal behavior, we tend to misinterpret the tribal behavior of others, especially those senior to us. When we made a point of spending the Christmas party with our team instead of the management group we want to join, we showed disdain for the way Tracy "sucked up" to them all night long. When we didn't feel like getting up early to play golf with the general manager, we told ourselves it wasn't really part of doing the job. We even laughed at the new guy who was eager to take our place. Instead of making the effort to befriend that "asshole" in production who is always making it hard for our group to fill orders, we wrote memos to the boss about her and openly showed our animosity toward her. Rather than being a conduit between our team and the rest of the organization, we were often a barrier between them and the organization.

There is a curious contradiction to the way a Sergeant Major sees tribal behavior. Where the tribe is built closely around the immediate job at hand, we seem to spontaneously value the tribe. When there is a separation between the tribal behavior and the work, we tend to disdain such activity. Even when we plateaued in our careers, we failed to see that the activities we defined as inappropriate or as non-work were part of other people's successful tribal behavior, part of managing the relationships that determine what will get done, who will do it and who will get credit for it. When the people who dedicated time to the tribal activity we scorned did get ahead, we still dismissed their success; "It's not what you know; it's who you know." What we failed to see was that our skewed abilities to operate in the tribal organization limited not only our advancement, but even our ability to do our job.

Become an "Ethnographer" of Your Tribes

This leads to the main point that makes the tribal organization important to the Sergeant Major:

*Your **job** may progress on bureaucratic lines,*

*But your **career** progresses on tribal lines*

As I have noted at several points in this chapter, the challenge is not to merely see tribal behavior, but to remove the negative lens through which you have viewed it. In anthropology, ethnographers are the kind of researchers who spend three years sitting under a tree in Fiji watching the people, then write a book about Fijian customs and norms. They do not write about what is good or bad about Fiji, but try to be as descriptive as possible, so that a reader can get a better understanding of what it means to be a Fijian. If you want to better understand the tribal behaviors that govern your work life, try to think more ethnographically. Focus on describing, not judging.

To help yourself remain descriptive, restrict yourself to the six questions a good ethnographer, or perhaps a newspaper reporter, can ask:

- Who?
- What?
- When?
- Where?
- How?
- Why?

These questions will help you to map the operations of the tribal organization. Be especially careful , though, with the "why?" question. This is a good answer:

"One reason Jane may have been promoted is that she has made herself visible to senior management at social functions."

This is not:

"Jane is a shameless self-promoter and a door mat for her boss".

An ethnographer does not follow a rigidly structured observational process, but takes notes as they occur, while trying to be as open as possible to what is going on in the environment. By reviewing these notes, he or she gradually develops ideas about relationships. Eventually, these relationships can be seen as patterns of meaning, showing how the culture operates. The following list offers some questions you might use to investigate the "foreign" tribes among which you work. Feel free to add other questions as they occur to you.

BECOMING AN ETHNOGRAPHER OF YOUR ORGANIZATION

- **Mapping the tribes:** What are the tribes in your territory? Feel free to name them if that helps. Who belongs to each tribe? What are their boundaries? What do the tribes value? How does one become a member or get expelled? Who acts as messenger between the tribes? Go back to the six questions above and ask them about the tribes.

- **Studying a Role Model:** Pick one person who you see as being favored by the company, a golden child who seems to be getting ahead rapidly. It is likely this will be somebody you dislike. Put that aside; your job is to understand, not to approve or disapprove. Map this person's success. Where did they start in the company? Where have the gone since then? What has contributed to their advancement? Who are their friends? What are their connections? Go back to the six questions and try to be as complete as possible about mapping this person's tribal connections. *Remember: You are likely to over-value direct work experience. Try to be conscious of this and include all factors, especially tribal ones.*

- **Comparison lists:** Make a list of several people you consider excellent who are making poorer progress in their careers than you think they should. Five is a good number, but use fewer or more if you find it useful. Then select an equivalent number you consider to be advancing faster than their abilities merit.
    - Compare the two lists. How do the tribal behaviors of the one group differ from those of the other? Ask the six questions and be as comprehensive as possible.
    - Now, what is the connection between the tribal behavior of each group and their advancement or their difficulties? Describe, don't judge.

- **Other ideas:** Don't be limited by these suggestions. They are intended to get you started. Feel free to ask yourself other questions about your tribal organization as they occur to you.

This exercise serves two purposes. First, of course, it is intended to help you better understand the tribal organization so that you can deal more effectively with it. The second point is to help you get into the habit of observing the tribal behavior that affects your career more descriptively and less judgmentally. Many Sergeant Majors who are observant enough to see this behavior and intelligent enough to understand it, are handicapped in dealing with it by our attitudes. Before we can move into the next chapter and start working on dealing with tribal behavior, it is necessary to take a step back from our negative feelings, to look with as cool a head as possible at how the tribal organization operates.

Summing Up

Every organization has two aspects, the bureaucratic and the tribal. If you are a Sergeant Major, there is a good chance you have relied too much on the power of the bureaucratic organization while ignoring or dismissing the operation of the tribal organization. Both aspects are necessary for organizational success and mastering both organizations is necessary for your success. The tribal organization is governed by the "hidden rulebook" that you have overlooked. Learning how tribal relationships operate in your work life can help you to stop playing by the wrong rulebook and start moving flexibly from bureaucratic to tribal rules as the situation demands. This will take practice. Perhaps the hardest challenge will be to stop judging tribal relationships negatively and to learn to describe them objectively. As you become more comfortable identifying tribal relationships and their operation, you will become better able to successfully negotiate them to achieve your goals. As we move into part two, this will be our focus.

PART TWO: SO YOU'RE A SERGEANT MAJOR. WHAT ARE YOU GOING TO DO ABOUT IT?

It is important to understand the characteristics of a Sergeant Major, where they come from, how they play out in organizational settings and what consequences they have. That has been the focus of chapters one through four. But understanding is not enough. We need to know how to manage our destiny, how to build the careers we want. To continue with the military analogy, we need to learn how to pull ourselves up by our own bootstraps. Let's summarize the main points so far:

- Your career difficulties are not unique. There are millions of Sergeant Majors like us out there.

- It is not our fault that we are Sergeant Majors, but it is our responsibility to decide what to do about it.

- We have failed to recognize that getting promoted is a separate job from doing our work tasks. We have worked on the latter at the expense of the former.

- As a consequence, our lack of progress may have been for good reason. We may have been disruptive to our organizations when we thought we were being valuable.

- We have often been playing from the wrong rulebook because we did not understand that organizations are tribal, as well as bureaucratic.

The following chapters offer a plan for using this understanding to take control of our careers. In short: thriving in our careers requires that we reflect on where we find meaning in our lives and how to integrate work in a satisfying and sustainable way. In order to find positive meaning and positive outcomes at work, we need to focus on building positive relationships. In order to do this, we must become more aware of how we communicate meaning to others. Once we better understand this, we can take positive steps to manage communication and relationships in a way that is personally meaningful.

Chapter five outlines the three career paths a Sergeant Major can choose. Chapter six is about getting our heads in the right place, as we attempt to develop a balanced relationship with our organization. In chapter seven, we turn to the difficult, but achievable, task of building more positive tribal work relationships. Chapter eight pulls it all together with a discussion of how to successfully market ourselves (yes, your career is a "product").

In sum, the chapters in this section are intended to redirect you from over-emphasis on your job to a more balanced emphasis on both the job of doing your work and the job of "doing" your career.

CHAPTER 5:
THE THREE BIG CAREER OPTIONS

~ツ~

Ok, you're a Sergeant Major and you want to build a successful career. There are three paths you can follow:

1. Thrive as a Sergeant Major
2. Advance in the organization
3. Become self-employed

These are the only likely paths. Even if you were to change careers, you would have the same three paths facing you. It is very important that you consciously choose one of these three options because they are mutually exclusive; if you are working on one you are working against the other two. A Sergeant Major who does not learn to successfully follow one of these paths, is likely to reach an early career plateau and receive increasingly impossible assignments on the inexorable path to "special projects," or the equivalent, until being cut loose in the next restructuring or downsizing. I have followed that path, as have several of my friends. I do not recommend it.

Your choice of paths will also influence how you should read the rest of this book. In writing it, I have given primary attention to those who wish to advance from Sergeant Major to the organizational "officer corps" of management. If, however, your choice is to thrive as a Sergeant Major, you will still need to deal with the same problems using a similar set of tools. You will, however, direct your efforts toward preventing your position from becoming toxic with the problems of the Sergeant Major Syndrome. Even if you choose self-employment, you will find that you must understand and deal with the Sergeant Major in you in order to be successful. Let's consider the relative merits of each option so you have a better idea of how you want to proceed.

Thrive as a Sergeant Major

Getting "Ahead"?

For many in the workforce, especially many Americans, "getting ahead" has become deeply embedded in our thinking about career. Ahead of what? One thing you don't want to get ahead of is yourself. I have worked in quite a range of jobs, from washing cars for a dollar an hour to management consulting for a couple thousand dollars a day. I have been the manager, the employee, the owner, the professional contractor. Of all these jobs, my favorite was the one I had as a team leader doing internal software support and maintenance programming. We were the contact of last resort for our field support people. We only got the problems nobody else could solve and when we solved them, as we inevitably did, we had grateful field people and clients singing our praises. I voluntarily worked a couple extra hours a day because I was so happy at work. I was highly valued by my organization. My co-workers were also my circle of friends. Life was good, until...

Convinced that I needed to get "ahead", I finished an MBA and got a position in entry level management. To this day, I have never again had a work situation I liked nearly as much as that team leader position. I'm not even sure that my getting "ahead" has resulted in much more money. I have a nominally higher income now, but if I consider the cost of additional education, unemployment and protracted periods of being a full-time student, I don't know how much financial gain "ahead" has brought. If I had it all to do over, there is an excellent chance I would try to thrive as a Sergeant Major in that team leader position. So what if I never advanced? I had good work, great co-workers, a sense of meaning and satisfaction in my job and enough money. These things are valuable.

Time Really Is Money and Vice Versa

And don't forget the value of time. Usually, "ahead" comes with a greater commitment of time to the job, often a 24/7 commitment. Every evening, every weekend day that you can devote to your life instead of your job has value. You don't even have to be at work for the job to take your time. If you're at the kids' Saturday soccer game and your head's in that problem you have to solve Monday—you're at work, bunkie! Before thinking about the greater authority and the greater income, don't forget to ask yourself what price the extra commitment is worth to you. After all, it isn't just minutes and hours the job is taking; it's your life. As Thoreau said, you can't kill time without injuring eternity.

Doing What You Like and Vice Versa

There are many good Sergeant Major jobs for individual contributors and team leaders. Perhaps you like having the hottest sales team in the company. Maybe you're the only wizard who understands the micro-code for the new computer. You may be an actuary, a lawyer, a professor; one of any number of technical specialists who enjoy working on the problems your expertise has trained you to solve. Don't forget that if you "advance" from this position, you are likely to do less and less of the problem-solving you like and more and more of the administrative paperwork and interpersonal work that you may dislike.

Can I Stop Reading Now?

Okay, suppose I've convinced you to remain a Sergeant Major. Is the rest of the book now inapplicable? No. Notice that this section is about how to "thrive" as a Sergeant Major, not merely how to survive. If you started reading in the first place, I assume you weren't exactly thriving. There is a big difference between being a successful Sergeant Major and being a victim of the Sergeant Major Syndrome. Remaining a Sergeant Major does not mean it is okay to exhibit the qualities listed in chapter two. Thriving means being valued in your position. Thriving means being able to get a succession of increasingly satisfying projects. It means building sustainable relationships both within your team and between your team and the larger organization. If you are to do that as well as possible, everything in this book is relevant.

If you want a cautionary example of failing to thrive, read Tracy Kidder's, *The Soul of a New Machine*. In it, a group of Sergeant Majors are sent on a suicide mission. After working against the organization, with insufficient resources, this group does the impossible and produces a new computer. Then, as Kidder describes what happens to each key member of the product team, we see them succumbing to the Sergeant Major Syndrome. They burn out, quit, experience family problems due to their skewed work/life balance; they get transferred to other, more impossible projects, all the while questioning why they bother to do this at all. This is surviving, if that. It is not thriving.

Advancing in the Organization

As obvious as it may sound, one thing easily forgotten by those who wish to advance is that once you leave the team/project role, you will have a different kind of job. This is not necessarily signaled by the first promotion from team member to team leader. You are still working on a project and, although you may have more meetings or paperwork, you are still tangibly connected to the outcomes that are real to you: the new software, the customer, the technical task.

Welcome to "Muddle Management"
In your next promotion, into middle management, you will leave behind the world you knew. This can be exciting; it can be growth for you—but, only if it fits your personality and career goals. Middle management is well named. Most of the things you will work on started someplace else and don't end with you. You have to get used to being a link in a chain. Your job relies on your ability to communicate and negotiate, to attend meetings, to build relationships—to live in a world you may have thought of until now as management bullshit.

Can you value the work of middle management? If not, go back to option one or forward to number three. There is an inflexible rule you will have to observe about the tribal rituals of your organization if you want to advance:

You can't just be *willing* to participate; you have to do it *enthusiastically!*

Think seriously about this. Then think about it again. Then some more! If this weren't a challenge to who and what you are as a human being, you wouldn't be reading this book. Sergeant Majors can usually empathize with the long-time slogan of Hebrew National kosher meats, "We answer to a higher authority." When following the rules leads in the direction of getting the work done, Sergeant Majors are the first to fall into line. When the rules seem to be a barrier to getting the work done, we tend to consistently value the work over the organization. But where project needs conflict with broader organizational strategy, plans or initiatives, good middle managers side with the organization. Can you?

Working For, Not Just In, the Organization

As Sergeant Majors, we tend to freely give ourselves permission to follow the spirit of the rules instead of the letter, subverting petty policy to serve what we see as the company's overall interest. If we want to advance, we have to learn that, with rare exceptions, following the rules, right or wrong *is* in the company's overall interest. We have to stop deciding for ourselves when our superiors should be listened to and when we should add our two cents' worth. It is not enough to be willing to follow the director's asinine plan; we have to actually show support for it. We cannot append snide comments to the new policy memo to show our people we really know what's going on; we have to be entirely behind the new policy. We have to eliminate behaviors that send the message that we're cooler, on a higher plane from or divergent from others. You know what I mean:

- The time you came to the "country club casual" event wearing sandals and cut off jeans instead of chino slacks and a shirt with a little alligator embroidered on it.

- That parody memo you wrote spoofing the new time-booking policy. everybody thought it was hilarious, but you were noticed putting management down.

- The coffee cup on your desk that reads "None of us is as stupid as all of us" [available from Despair.com—not that you need my help finding subversive material].

If you want to advance, you have to make up your mind; can the company depend on you to support it 100% or can't it? Unfortunately, we have a word for people who are dependable 99% of the time. We call them undependable. If you are merely willing to try middle management, but you see it as selling your soul, your chances of succeeding are nil. The only way you are likely to be able to advance in management is if you are capable of seeing management and the organization positively.

Is It Worth It?

Look deep into your soul. I mean it. There is no point in a bird deciding to become a dog. If you are going to work your tail off to advance in the organization, then undermine yourself by showing through your behavior, attitude and artifacts that you reserve the right to support the company only when you approve of it, save yourself a ton of aggravation and don't make the effort in the first place. In later chapters, we will talk about how you can learn to better play the role of middle manager, but none of the advice will work unless you can see that role as genuinely worthwhile. If playing this role is inconsistent with keeping your self-respect, move forward or backward one section. You are better suited either to thrive as a Sergeant Major or for self-employment.

Becoming Self-Employed

If You Are Doing Well at Home...

I am fond of the Ted Turner dictum to "lead, follow or get the hell out of the way." We have covered the two options for following and, unless you are independently wealthy, you can't afford to get out of the way. The only option left is to lead, to run your own show. This section is a bit long because, while self-employment can be richly rewarding for some, it is a crushing disappointment to many others. In his essay, "Life Without Principle", Thoreau quotes the following advice for gold-seeking adventurers from a guidebook of the period, "If you are doing well at home: stay there". I became self-employed at

21 and went bankrupt. It scarred me for half my working life. I started a business at 50 that was highly successful and which I sold for a large profit after only thirty months—it scarred me too. I have seen both sides of self-employment. Consider Thoreau's advice carefully.

You'll notice that I don't call this section "entrepreneurship". If you want a book that romanticizes entrepreneurship, buy one of the thousands available from the many who have not experienced it or the few who have succeeded. Edison was right, success really is 1% inspiration and 99% perspiration. This does not mean you should forego considering self-employment. It means you should consider it with a healthy respect for the hard slog and risk it will involve. When I owned a successful group of coffee shops in Sedona, Arizona, a customer once asked me, "Was it always your dream to own a coffee shop?" I replied, "It has never been any part of any of my dreams—and that's probably why we're successful."

If you do go into business for yourself, remember that your first employee will be a Sergeant Major—you. It will become essential to understand and work with your "inner Sergeant Major" because there is now no organizational officer corps to provide structure. Just as you will start out being both the boss and your first exploited employee, you must learn to be both a good Sergeant Major and the officer to whom you report.

Seven Questions to Ask Yourself

Here are some of the most important things to consider if you think self-employment might be for you:

CONSIDERING SMALL BUSINESS?

1. What is your product/market/volume model?
2. What is your personality?
3. What is your family situation?
4. What is the risk; are you prepared to take it?
5. Are you prepared for the initial sacrifice?
6. Where will the money come from?
7. What new skills will be demanded of you?

What is Your Product/Market/Volume Model?

It's amazing how many people go into business without asking themselves who will buy their goods or services. If you are to succeed, you must answer three questions:

- What will I sell?
- Who will buy it and why?
- How many sales do I have to make to be profitable and where will they come from?

A surprising number of people sell what they love and assume everyone else cares as much about the product as they do. You have to think like the customer. If I want a Christmas doll for my toddler, I am unlikely to have much interest in the hand-painted collectible you want to sell me for $1,500. For your part, if you can make the doll for $600 and sell it for a $900 markup, that's a very respectable profit, but if you only make eight sales a year, your store will soon be up for lease. Unless you have a clear idea who your customers are, know why your product appeals to them *from the perspective of their values and interests*, and have a plan to make enough sales to become profitable before you go broke, consider remaining employed by somebody else.

What Is Your Personality?

Successful business people tend to share certain personality qualities. Self-confidence is important. So is an orientation toward activity, toward getting things done. Reflective people and sensitive people are at a disadvantage. Most of all, it is important that the hard work and pressure fill you with a sense of challenge, that they inspire rather than crush you. Take a little time to do an online search for "personality + entrepreneur". You will find many resources to help you think about whether you and self-employment are a compatible match.

What Is Your Family Situation?

It is one thing to risk everything you have. It is quite another to risk everything a loved one has. Give some thought to the downside risk: If you try and fail, will it unfairly hurt anyone you're responsible for?

Does the financial risk endanger your ability to pay the mortgage, care for aged parents, provide the things you want your children to have? If you're about to make a step of this magnitude, you won't want to dwell long on the possibility of failure, but it is irresponsible to simply assume things will work out for you. They may, or they may not.

Even if you are successful from day one, most business startups absorb a huge portion of the owner's time. When you're working the 28 hour days, will your family be supportive? Do you think it's acceptable to miss Debbie's ball game and Mike's school play? How will your marriage respond to your devotion to the work—on top of the financial pressure and emotional volatility you are bringing to it?

Family dependents can have a positive motivational effect if they give you a reason to succeed and the pride of having gotten to a better place for them and with them. It is equally possible that you will find yourself in the impossible position of being asked to give more to them and more to the business, when you are already giving all that you have to both. Think carefully about this. If you still think it's a good idea, discuss it with everyone involved. Not only do they have the right to be consulted, you are well advised not to jump off the high board unless you have strong family support.

What Is the Risk and Are You Prepared to Take It?
All business startups are risky, but some involve more risk than others. I once started a café. In that area, fewer than 10% of all startups last two years. On the other hand, I once worked for a guy who left his job as a finance professor and started a consulting business when a major client gave him a six-figure (in today's dollars) contract. That was risky, but far less so. I know another guy who made his fortune in a high tech startup where his former employer provided the funding and had a buy-back agreement if the product was successful. This held minimal risk because even if the venture failed, my friend would have lost somebody else's money and would still be highly employable in his industry. What level of risk would you face? Can you accept that?

Another element of risk is the customer base. Can you survive on one customer? A dozen? A hundred? In my café business, I needed two thousand sales a week from the day I opened. There is no simple rule that more or fewer customers is more difficult to manage, but the fewer customers you have, the more information you can get, which reduces risk. If you need six consulting clients, you can research organizations, talk individually to potential clients and learn what stands between you and success. If you want to open a retail store in a mall where the rent is expensive and the average sale is eight dollars, you need about a squillion customers. It's much harder to assess whether they will appear and the risk is harder to determine.

If you have your downside covered by investors, those same investors are going to want a large piece of your success and a large voice in the business. Can you avoid risk without becoming *their* Sergeant Major? The more you have relationships you can build on with customers/clients, the more you can control risk. The bottom line is what do you stand to lose if things go belly-up?

- your savings?
- your credit?
- your home?
- your employability?
- your family?

Note that you may be gambling your past (savings, assets), your present (home, lifestyle) and/or your future (credit rating, employability). Think about it. This isn't a time to say, "What the hell." This is a time to list what you can lose, to try to assess the chances of losing it and then asking yourself with a cool head if you are ready to face that loss.

Are You Prepared for the Initial Sacrifice?
At a coffee trade show I attended several years ago, a former aircraft engineer who now owns a group of cafés in Seattle once described self-employment as a "rock crusher." I agree. On the upside, it can grind off the inessential parts of you to show you who you really are. On the downside, it can just as readily crush you into dust. When I went into business with my ex-wife, she had never run a retail intensive, small-ticket, service business. I had grown up in

one, working for my father. When our business opened, we both got hit equally with the tsunami of work and stress. The difference was that I had expected it and it was a surprise to her. Pretty soon our mom-and-pop enterprise was a "pop" enterprise as she found hourly work from another employer.

Even if you are wildly successful in your new enterprise, you are likely to have a prolonged period of intense work compounded by intense stress. Working 24/7 doesn't quite describe it. It's more like working 28/8. One of the ways being the boss differs from being an employee is that excuses don't matter and there are few second chances. If you stop at the point where nobody could blame you for quitting, you'll have a face-saving explanation for losing—but you'll lose. I don't know of a single startup business owner who does not have one or more stories about what they did when there was absolutely no way forward, but they went forward anyway. The time will most definitely come when you are faced with failure and have no options. Are you prepared to do whatever is necessary when that time comes?

Where Will the Money Come From?
There are only three ways to get money and they're all bad. In business school they talk about debt, equity and funds from operations. It sounds neat and clean. It isn't.

In a startup, you don't have any funds from operations yet, so that boils down to what you can afford to put into the business. If you put less in, others will get more of the profit if you're successful. If you put more in, you stand to lose more if you're not.

Debt means going to the bank, or to anybody who will offer you money with a fixed repayment schedule. I like debt because as long as you pay the bankers each month, they shut up and leave you alone. They don't want to run your business. The downside is that in good months and bad, you have to pay them regardless. If you have a few lean months, they *will* run your business. David Dunbar Buick died broke because the bankers kicked him out of one of the most profitable auto companies in history. Willie Durant, who founded General Motors was booted by the bankers and spent three years fighting his way back in. Henry Ford…well, you get the idea.

Equity means trading a share of the business for money, either by taking on partners or selling stock shares. The nice thing about equity is that when the business makes no money, you owe your equity partners nothing, but this flexibility comes at a high price. For one thing, unlike bankers, equity partners are never paid off. They get a share of the business forever. In addition, a share of the business gives equity partners a voice. They get to second guess your decisions. A Sergeant Major is especially unlikely to welcome this input. If all partners share a common vision of the business, or if partners bring in expertise you need, this can be good, but don't count on it to happen. People who want to turn resources into goods and services for customers don't live in the same world as people who want to turn money into more money. Managing investors is tricky at best.

This does not, of course, mean that you cannot successfully combine these three sources. It just means that it is about as tricky as juggling chain saws. Give serious thought to where the money is going to come from and what that means in terms of repayment risk, profit sharing and sharing of authority. Then ask yourself how this challenges you as a Sergeant Major.

What New Skills Will Be Demanded of You?
This is the easiest point to overlook and it is probably the most important. The Sergeant Major going into self-employment is freed from the need to deal with management, but only by *becoming* management. There is truth to the platitude that nobody works for as unreasonable a boss as the self-employed.

There is only one thing you have to do well to be successful in a small business startup—everything! That means you are now the head of accounting, the marketing manager, the keeper of the strategic vision, the human resource department, the first temporary worker called when there is a staff shortage—and maybe the window cleaner as well. One luxury the employed Sergeant Major has is the ability to stay focused on the team, leaving the rest of the organization to the rest of the organization. With self-employment, that privilege disappears. This presents two challenges.

First, you will need to learn the content of all these areas, at least enough to know if you are being well served. You may not do the books, but you have to know if your bookkeeping and accounting are in order. That means learning enough accounting to know the difference between being in order and being in disarray. The same holds true of advertising, staffing, taxes… Even in sales or product development, your most likely strong area, if you think like a team leader, you may need to expand your skills. The game is no longer about your project; it is about the entire process, from sourcing to servicing a satisfied customer. In most cases, this involves thinking about parts of the value chain that precede and follow the limited portion that constitutes any discrete project. Some parts of this chain will be in your company; some will be outside it. This leads to the second challenge.

As difficult as it is to learn the content knowledge your business requires, for a Sergeant Major it will be even more difficult to learn the *relational* skills you need in order to bring all the parts together. As I've said, you have not been freed of management by entering self-employment; you have become management. In becoming the employer, you have changed your power base, which will be an advantage, but you will still have to deal with the same relationship demons that haunt the employed Sergeant Major.

For instance, when you are holding the checkbook, you always have the power to say, "This meeting is over and I won't be dealing with you," but that power will take you less far than you think. Yes, you will have choices of who to rely on as suppliers and vendors, who to hire as employees, what strategies and terms to deal with in seeking customers. You will, however, seldom be in a position to make a unilateral demand:

- **It is always good to suck up to creditors.** Bankers, landlords (and shareholders if you have them) have power over you. You want them happy—you *re-eally* want them happy. There is always a way to void a lease. There is always the chance that you will need to borrow more money or seek relief during times of hardship. The technical term for small business people who take a stand against their creditors is "roadkill."

- **What's the second word in the phrase "supplier *relationships*"?** Yes, you can choose who will be a supplier.

This gives you leverage. But sometimes you have few choices. If only one or a couple of suppliers can meet your needs, you don't have to burn too many bridges before you have no bridges left. No matter how many suppliers you have, the quality of your relationship is going to influence not just the price, but the quality of the goods or services, the dependability of the supply and your ability to work together to deal with the ever-changing competitive landscape.

- **Slave labor can only perform simple tasks.** You pay your employees and that would seem to give you the power to say, "We'll do it this way because I want to." Legally it does, but so what? If you're building a pyramid, you might get the construction done this way, but when the worker has any discretion in how to do a job, you have to figure out how to get them to *want* to do it well. This is going to inevitably come down to showing qualities like respect, trust, honesty and willingness to work collaboratively. Giving commands is unlikely to get you where you're going. You have to manage employee relationships.

- **Be indispensible to your customers/clients.** With very rare exceptions, your customers don't need you. Merely making yourself available to them won't help you even if you do have a good solution to a legitimate problem. You only have customers when *they* see the problem as needing solving and they see you as the solution. Good products often die. Bad products often succeed. You can influence this, but you don't get to decide. Product quality is another influence, but not a decisive one (BetaMax; Lotus 1,2,3; WordPerfect…). Customer choice is the only factor determining life and death for you. That leaves you with one more set of critical relationships you can't command.

Many successful businesspeople either were or would have been Sergeant Majors if they had worked for somebody else, but they did not become successful using the same skill set that made them excellent technical people. They did not manage their business relationships the way a Sergeant Major is likely to deal with the rest of his or her company. They either learned these skills or brought in others to deal with them. If you are considering self-employment, I suggest you ask yourself two sets of questions. The first set is the seven questions discussed in this chapter. Once you have done that, ask yourself, how your inner Sergeant Major will deal with the demands of self-employment—then read chapters six through eight.

Summing Up

As a Sergeant Major, you have three general paths to career success: thrive as a Sergeant Major, advance in the organization, or become self-employed. Each presents significant challenges and opportunities. None is better than the other except in relationship to what you want from your career, what your personality and skills are, and what you are willing and able to work on as you develop. This is a question of which path is the best fit for you.

It is also a question of working smart. If you want to thrive as a Sergeant Major, you have to recognize and change the things that marginalize you. If you want to advance in the organization, you won't get ahead merely by doing the things that allow you to thrive in the job you're already in. If you belong to the minority who will find success in self-employment, by all means, stop banging your head against the brick wall of employment—but be very careful to consider if this really is for you. *You can only get what you work for if you do work that leads where you want to go.* In the following chapters, I turn in more detail to the question of how you can do just that.

CHAPTER 6:
BALANCING YOUR COMMITMENT TO WORK

I t is reasonable for you to look for meaning in life. People are meaning makers. We find meaning innumerable ways, but we must find it. Meaning is foundational to a successful life. It is also reasonable that we expect work to contribute to that meaning. After all, you devote a lot of your waking life to it. The operative phrase here is "contribute to." If work is your ultimate source of meaning, you are almost certain to be disappointed. Once again, we have to face that word so heinous to a good Sergeant Major, "balance".

Balancing the Menu

I recently consulted to a woman who was responsible for a hospitality program that trains chefs. Part of what we dealt with was the alienation experienced by several of the staff. In general, these were people who had considerable ability and experience running their own kitchen in restaurants and hotels. Although they had become educators, they still thought like chefs, which made them classic Sergeant Majors. One way this was reflected was in their tendency to do their best according to their individual standards, then to blame the organization for failing to value them on their terms. One of the things I talked about with their manager was the problem of motivating them and aligning their efforts, with each other and with the needs of the department.

Now, if we read the management literature, we might think that motivation is primarily a problem of getting unwilling people to do what we want them to. That may be true in the factory (where the theory originated), but the majority of the workforce today is more like these chefs in that we *want* to do the work. We care about what we do. But we tend to want to do it our personal way, which is not helpful to an organization. When this is the case, a manager has two main challenges. The first is to support the worker rather than to use traditional carrot-and-stick methods of motivation. It is necessary to recognize that succeeding at the task and being recognized for it is the most motivating thing to the worker. The second challenge is to align everyone's work so that the group works together and not for divergent, individual goals.

As part of my engagement, I had spoken with these chefs and it had become clear to me that they felt passionately about sharing their skills with students. They arrived early, worked late and spent a great deal of time—like good Sergeant Majors—finding "guerrilla" solutions that would permit them to get things done where organizational systems failed to support them. I respected these guys a great deal and I hope that my engagement contributed to their getting better support for their efforts from the organization.

At the same time, I also discussed with the manager that if these guys were trying to find the meaning of their life at work, work was always going to come up short. With rare exceptions, people who need their work in order to have meaning in their life are troublesome employees. They make good suicide bombers and cult members. Don't drink the Kool Aid.

It IS reasonable to want work that has meaning.

It is NOT reasonable to expect most jobs to be your primary source of meaning.

I am not going to discuss this in terms of "workaholism," a term that is applied all too casually to anyone who works hard. Work as hard as you like, with my blessing. My own father worked a minimum of seventy hours a week, but his meaning was centered on family, not on the business. I never fully appreciated this until I went into business myself and was working a seven day week. I once said to him, "You know, Dad, I used to admire the fact that you were willing to work so hard for the family. Now I admire the fact that you took Sundays off!" His simple reply says it all: "Well, I had children."

Sources of Meaning

I have spent a great deal of time reflecting on where people find meaning in social life. I think that in virtually all cases it comes from a combination of six sources: God, wealth, career, family, community and avocation. By "avocation", I mean our spare time interests, anything from trout fishing to working for the city mission. These six sources of meaning can be negative as well as positive. Our religious beliefs can torment us with guilt. Family abuse can haunt us. We can feel rootless and disconnected from community.

Take a bit of time to reflect on the role of these six sources of meaning in your life. Using the table below, score the positive or negative contribution each makes to your sense of having a meaningful life. Where does career stand? Unless you have a positive score from the other five without career included, you may be trying to find meaning in your work life that cannot be provided there.

MEANING: THE BIG SIX

	Negative					Positive				
	-5	-4	-3	-2	-1	0	1	2	3	4	5
God											
Wealth											
Avocation											
Family											
Community											
Career											

Notice that career can contribute to all of the other five. Tom Monaghan, the founder of Domino's Pizza, used his wealth to further his religious beliefs (God). Oprah Winfrey uses her organization and a portion of her wealth to help empower women and poor people (avocation). But career *as career* is a different thing. You can't sell enough spa pools or design enough new microchips to give meaning to an otherwise meaningless life.

What Becomes of the Broken Hearted?

Let's go back to the chefs I mentioned above. What was happening to them? They were breaking their backs doing things that were not expected of them. Because these things were not expected, they were not rewarded. Because the activities were not done as part of the group, there was little appreciation from others because there was little understanding of what efforts had been made. As a result, the few people in this position increasingly came to see the organization as persecuting them while seeing themselves as defending program quality against student ignorance, against lack of senior management support, against lack of appreciation by the local community, government, God and the universe. As a consequence, they became increasingly negative, defensive, hard to collaborate with and hard to support.

They Came to Be Dominated by Their Anger

I find situations like this especially sad. This is not a case of an oppressive employer trying to screw the worker to the wall. It's a case where the employer and employee start with a common goal and, in the pursuit of that goal, end up at odds, with both suffering, along with the work. There is much responsibility on the employer's side to provide the supports such employees need, but that is not what we are presently looking at. The employee—these chefs, me, perhaps you—becomes a martyr to a cause that does not need martyrs and most or all of the good-faith effort is lost. In large part, we can see that the trouble these guys encountered emerged from the fact that they were working for themselves, following orders they alone had issued

You Can't be Significantly Better Than Your Organization

If we wish to achieve a balanced perspective on our work, we might heed the advice I once received from an Indian friend much influenced by the teachings of Gandhi that, "In order to change the world, you must first survive." Sergeant Majors frequently hold ourselves to standards that are not met around us. Then, we tend to judge others as deficient rather than trying to adapt to the norm. We need to adjust our sights. Before we can do that, we need to learn to deal with the anger we have permitted ourselves as a way of dealing with frustration.

If you are a Sergeant Major, you may often think the standards of your organization are pretty shabby. You may sometimes be right. Other times, you will be holding it to unrealistic standards. Whether you are right or not is unimportant. What matters is that *your organization is what it is; no more, no less.*

If you think delivery standards are slack and you want to make sure your customers get better service, you are taking on responsibility for the entire order fulfilment process. If you want your scanner component for the new photocopier to be higher quality than the components being delivered by the other project teams, you are wasting your efforts on quality that will not deliver customer value and unnecessarily increasing your company's cost of production. You are making life tougher for yourself—and, in all likelihood, others—without making it better for anyone.

I once had a conversation with an academic colleague who was (justifiably) horrified by the grading standards at our institution. Despite the fact that a great many students who were admitted were unable to successfully master the course material, the grading standard was that there would be a certain percentage range of A grades, a certain range of B's etc. Her position was that she would make sure a student getting an A met her standards so that employers could know that it was a real A on that student's transcript. My position was that, as much as it pained me, I was going to follow school policy because employers would not know that a grade was from me. They would not know a "real A" from any other A. They would only know, in general, what a graduate of my institution was worth.

My colleague was trying to be better than the institution. I shared her standards and empathized, but could see no way she could achieve that goal. Over the subsequent years, she did not achieve any personal increase in educational quality, but burned herself out fighting the system. That is the invariable fate of anyone who tries to be significantly better than their organization—and it doesn't change things if you are right!

Remember the thought from Wilfred Bion mentioned in chapter four—as soon as a group forms, its primary purpose becomes the protection of the group. When you diverge from the group, it doesn't matter whether you're a high-end or low-end outlier. All that matters is that you're buggering up the normal manner of operation. Think of a team of trapeze artists. It doesn't matter if one of them is early or late getting into position. What matters is that they weren't there for the others.

Mind you, it is possible to think about changing employers. There are, of course, organizations which perform better than others. You might be able to move up from a loser to a winner. But be careful! ***Organizations are inefficient and Sergeant Majors tend to be unforgiving of that!*** All organizations have to rely on procedures that can be carried out by the average applicant, with regular employee turnover. They have to optimize conflicting market, financial, product and other goals. They are run by ordinary humans with the ordinary amount of myopia, self-interest and differences of values. If we expect the work day to be a rerun of *Guns of Navarone* or *Raid on Entebbe*, we are guaranteed to be disappointed. Organizing is about getting large groups of people to do things repetitively, dependably and predictably. This necessarily involves a level of formalization, policy—and mediocrity—that sticks in the craw of the average Sergeant Major, but which is essential for organizational survival.

Dealing with Our Anger

This situation makes you angry, doesn't it? Anger is both a symptom that our perspective is not balanced and a problem in its own right, keeping us from thinking and acting effectively. When the Sergeant Major's commitment to the organization is, in the Sergeant Major's eyes, unrequited, it most often has one of two results: anger or alienation. If I turn my negative feeling outward and remain engaged with the organization, they are expressed as anger. If I turn them inward and disconnect, I become a zombie, a living dead employee. In both cases, the challenge to me is the same. I have to first deal with the feelings that have put me in such a negative place. Then I have to manage my relationships with others so I can get out of it. Anger is a sign of imbalance. Balance, which we must cultivate, requires removing the anger.

Anger can have a positive role. Like any emotion, it can be an indication of a problem needing attention. Our challenge is to use anger as a tool rather than to be driven by it. If you are seen as an angry person, you will be shunned—sometimes so subtly that you are unaware of it. If you are angry, you are not making your best decisions. It doesn't matter if you have good reasons to be angry. The Sergeant Major who wants to thrive must stop looking for legitimate reasons to be angry and must start realizing that being angry is a disadvantage regardless of the reasons. Legitimate anger will work to your disadvantage as strongly as misplaced anger. To begin dealing with anger, remember two principles:

Forget about establishing that you were right in the first place.

Work toward getting the outcome you want instead of vindication.

I have often noticed that when I complain to a company about bad service, the reply I am likely to get will seek to establish, first, that there was nothing that could have been done about the problem I encountered and, second, that I am wrong, not they. What effect do you think this has on building a positive customer relationship for the future?

For instance, I recently stayed in a boutique hotel that I knew had a lovely old claw-footed bathtub in the room. My anticipation of having a leisurely bath was spoiled, though, by the fact that the hotel had booked my reservation and checked me in without telling me that they had no hot water! When I returned the customer service survey in my room, I indicated that I was unhappy about this and would be unlikely to stay there again unless the management sought to compensate me for this inconvenience.

The reply I received began by defending that there was no hot water available in that area due to city construction (not that I cared and besides, it was planned construction, not an emergency). It went on to say that I had obtained the room at a discount rate (which was true, but irrelevant. It was still fifty dollars more than a room I could have booked that did have hot water). They grudgingly offered me fifty dollars off on my next stay, which meant that I had to return and pay full fare before receiving any sort of compensation. As the customer, I don't have to convince them that I'm right. I will simply not stay there again. What have they accomplished for themselves?

In contrast, when I had my cafes, I once received a letter from a woman who complained about the service she received. Frankly, I thought she was being unfair, but her continuing business was not based on what I thought. I wrote back to her, thanking her for complaining. After all, I explained, we can only make things right when we know we have failed to satisfy somebody. The customer who complains gives us an opportunity that the customer who merely goes away unhappy does not. I then told her what had been done to assure that her problem would not recur: I had talked to the server about whom she complained and we had made a change to store procedure, which I explained in the letter. Finally, I apologized unconditionally to this woman, without making excuses, and offered her a gift certificate worth about three times the value of the purchase about which she had complained. This validated her desire for vindication, but it also gave her a risk-free incentive to return and experience good service. Not only did we keep her ongoing business, but we had increased our good word-of-mouth advertising in the community. She won, but was that a loss for us?

Did I want to explain to this woman that she was wrong, tell her how hard our jobs were and ask how well she would do if she had to serve custom orders to three hundred people a day? Of course I did. Was I hurt that she had not appreciated the business into which I was pouring my heart? Yes again. Was I going to gain anything by trying to convince the customer of this? Not on your life. I could defend my ego at the expense of the future business relationship or I could respect her ego and preserve the relationship. I had to choose whether to be right or to be successful. Sergeant Majors tend to choose being right.

In *The Soul of a New Machine*, Tracy Kidder tells the story of an engineer named Peck who had called a person outside the project group an asshole. To protect the group's access to the person who had been offended, Peck's boss ordered him to apologize. Peck went to the person he had insulted and said, "I'm sorry you're an asshole". If you're smiling as you read this and wishing you were Peck, you are reacting like a Sergeant Major. Even when we don't respond to others like this in so many words, we are accomplished in getting the point across.

Managing Anger
Make Emotions Your Servants
So, the first thing we have to do is to remember the advice of the Godfather, "It's just business." This is very difficult when one is angry. We need to start by trying to put things into perspective. The very first thing to remember when provoked is don't attack!

MANAGING ANGER

1. Make your emotions your servant, not your master
   - Don't attack
   - It's just business; it's not *jihad*.
   - Remember, the first person to lose their temper is the loser
   - Jerks will not reward you for proving they're jerks
   - Empathize; put yourself in their shoes
   - Try to laugh at it
2. Be pragmatic; find a solution
   - Don't seek pity; don't offer excuses
   - Focus on outcomes, not retribution
   - Ask yourself, "What outcome do I want from this?"
   - Ask, "What outcome do others want from this?"
   - Seek middle ground
   - Watch your language – *and* body language
3. Be seen as…
   - Having made a positive contribution
   - Being a peace maker, not a warrior
   - Being a solution, not a problem

Don't send that flaming e-mail. Don't speak when you are choked with rage. Don't say or do anything you will have to live down. Often, when something angers us, we lose before we have a chance to engage because of the belligerence of our initial reaction. If you have to leave the meeting, log off your computer, lock your office door, leave work early or hum Three Blind Mice until you are numb, don't respond until you can do so level-headedly. It is usually the case that the first person to lose their temper will be the loser, but even when the other person has lost their temper first, you still have the opportunity to turn things into a lose/lose. Don't do it. Go to your car if you need to scream—and stay there until you're done.

When Peck said, "I'm sorry you're an asshole," he crossed another line we need to learn to observe. In my experience, jerks will not reward you for attempting to show them that they are jerks. This remains true even if they are and especially so if your proof is conclusive. In fact, the more true it may be that we are dealing with an "asshole", the more important it becomes to treat that person with respect.

That won't be easy, but it is necessary. One way to become better at this is to try to empathize with our adversaries. We are more likely to be used to thinking of them as evil, stupid or malicious. But consider this: nobody does anything for reasons *they* consider bad. How would things look if you stood in your adversary's shoes? What values, what information lead this person to take the position that makes you angry? To the extent that you can appreciate the perspective that is leading this person to do what they are doing, you are in a position to work cooperatively with them to change things.

Now here's the final test of whether you have things in perspective: Can you laugh at it? I know it will hurt, but try it. Really, when the history of this century is written, will your crusade against that salesperson who keeps promising features you can't build make it into the textbooks? There is some truth to the platitude that nothing matters very much and very little matters at all. Take a deep breath; remember that the sun will rise tomorrow no matter how your work battles turn out, and try to smile.

Be Pragmatic; Find a Solution

Stop trying to show that you are right.

Start trying to achieve the right outcome.

When a Sergeant Major is trying to show a jerk what an idiot they are, the implied message is, *"You are a problem."* It is a positive step to be able to de-personalize that attitude to the statement, *"You caused this problem."* We must still take things one step further to, *"We have a problem."* The first two statements lead to blame and defense. Neither is productive. We need to be able to discuss the issue freely, put information on the table somewhat objectively and have some hope of getting all parties involved to participate in a solution. As long as your primary purpose is to show that you are right, this will be impossible. Forget about vindication; you won't get it anyway. The closest thing to vindication you can achieve is to succeed in reaching your goal.

Reaching your goal involves asking yourself what you want to achieve from this conflict. Are you too close to your work? If you have developed a degree of tunnel vision, that would be normal. Step back and look at the broader terrain. Can you move forward without winning the particular issue you are about to go to war over? Are you fighting to get a particular person assigned to your team when what you need is any person with a certain skill? Do you need Toyota to pilot your new database or do you simply need an organization of a certain size? Don't get locked into the specifics of the fight. Ask yourself what you need for a successful outcome. The best kind of argument is one you can go around.

Don't forget to ask what outcomes everyone else wants from this situation. Very often, you will find that what is most important to you is not what is most important to others. This is valuable information. If you can get what you care about most by sacrificing things you care less about, you've broken the stalemate. Often, everyone can win in this sense if a creative middle ground can be found where everyone sacrifices something, but all get most of what is important to them. Based on my work experience, I can confidently say that this will be true the majority of the time and it will contribute to a partial solution in virtually all cases.

Remember, finding an objective solution to the problem is only the bureaucratic side of your situation. The tribal context in which you are interacting must be negotiated successfully also. When you suggest a compromise that is sensitive to the values and needs of those you are opposing, you show respect for their reality. You show a willingness to work with their needs. You bring them into the situation as part of the solution, not as part of the problem. This often changes things dramatically.

Watch the Nonverbal Communication
Most of all, watch your language. This includes body language. Sergeant Majors generally have excellent skills for making sure people clearly understand the things they are *not* saying. If I think my manager's solution to the problem is asinine, there is a way of saying "Okay, let's go with that" which shows support and there's a way of saying exactly the same words while sending a clear message that I'm going along with an asinine plan because I have no choice. When you are dealing with others, it doesn't matter what you *said*. What matters is what the other person thinks you *mean*. There can be a world of difference.

If you want to solve problems by bringing others on board to collaborate, you have to focus on the meanings, not the words. For instance, if you're in marketing and your problem is that the products you're advertising have not been produced yet, when you sit down with production, the conversation is likely to start with the trading of blame. This is not constructive. Starting the conversation by describing the problem rather than telling production what they should have done offers more constructive possibilities. In the likely event that you are blamed for the situation, you have several options other than defense. You can apologise. You can say it isn't worth trying to work out who did what, but you're sure we have all done our best. You can make sure that throughout the meeting your language is about the facts and what to do with them. You might be amazed what this can accomplish.

By watching your language, you are doing more than simply applying communication skills. You are influencing feelings.

These feelings, in turn, determine the relationships of the tribal organization and those relationships determine what will happen with your project and your career. If you are to become effective in using language, stop thinking about what you are *saying* and start thinking about what *meaning* you are conveying. What matters is not what you say, but what they hear and what they hear matters less at the objective level, more at the level of feelings.

Rhetorical skills won't help you a lot in this case. What is needed is the ability to put yourself in the shoes of the person to whom you are speaking and to convey notions such as respect, friendliness, and tribal membership. I will return to this topic in chapter seven.

Being Seen Positively
Okay, the problem is solved and everyone has moved on. What residual feelings have you left behind from the way you handled it? This has two important consequences for you. First, how people feel about you based on this issue will color how they deal with you next time. Second, how you have been seen dealing with this issue will be important information for those who determine the path of your career. In both cases, you want to leave the same impression. You want people to think how positive and constructive you were in getting to a collaborative solution.

There is a saying in politics that friends come and go; enemies accumulate. You don't want this to be true in your organizational life. Maybe there was a time when you made your annual sales numbers by using leverage from your boss to get the credit department to extend terms to some financially weak clients. You got a good annual review while the credit department had to answer for the increase in accounts receivables times. You won that round, but they're gunning for you now. What will they be likely to do when you try to clear credit for a new account with a shaky credit history, but also with a large government contract? It's payback time, kiddo. Kiss that account good-bye.

Nothing in the prior example had to do with policy. The important relations were tribal. You used them to your advantage when you had your boss lean on the credit people. They used it to their advantage when they selectively used policy to keep you from making a good sale. Your informal standing in the tribal organization is your career capital. Whether you choose to thrive in your position or to advance, you will want to be able to rely on positive tribal relationships. Dealing with your anger as you encounter problems gives you an opportunity to greatly increase this capital, but this is an asset Sergeant Majors tend to overlook because it is intangible, informal and not part of the work task itself. Don't make this mistake.

Warrior or Diplomat?
Sergeant Majors tend to admire warriors. Organizational effectiveness tends to be the domain of the diplomats. This is important to remember when angry. It would be lovely to be a flaming sword in the hand of Truth and Justice, sweeping away the evildoers, but save that for video gaming. When you deal with conflict this way, you lose even when you get what you want. Sure, maybe the project reaches completion successfully, but everyone you smote like Jehovah is waiting for payback. Your superiors are looking at you as somebody who has to be contained, which works against advancement. Even your own work group may be uncomfortable with the way you got them to the goal.

Diplomats, on the other hand, are less visible, but more valued. Diplomacy has not always been my strong suit, but one time that it was successful and taught me a valuable lesson came early in my teaching career. I was made Acting Dean of a postgraduate program while my boss, the Dean, was on sabbatical. She was a person who saw the organization largely in terms of enemies, against whom one had to plot and guard. This included the Registrar and several people responsible for dealing with student problems. Upon taking the role of Acting Dean, my administrative assistant and I took three of the key people in this area to lunch—with no agenda other than to make a positive personal connection. When asked what our agenda was, we answered honestly and transparently that we wanted to get the year off on a positive foot. As the year progressed, we were amazed how these people and their staff routinely acted as our advocates. One simple act that was not directly work-related became one of the most important things I did that year to make the work possible.

Be the Solution, Not the Problem
Finally, as you try to decide what to do with your anger, think about dealing with it in a manner that leaves you being seen as a solution, not a problem. I accidentally fell into a situation that taught me an important lesson in this regard. Having taken a job as the senior member of a very undistinguished university department, I was horrified when my department head assigned me to do postgraduate advising under the "supervision" of a person who was herself still studying for her Ph.D. Over the following two years, a long series of unfortunate events led to a confrontation with this person in which I said a number of grossly inappropriate things. Perhaps the *least* offensive comment was along the lines of, "You have so little experience that you think you're in a real university teaching real postgraduate students." It went downhill from there.

That was on a Friday. On Monday I had planned to apologize for my remarks, but, by then, she had complained to the department head, so I had to meet with him. In that meeting, I began by apologizing and saying that there was no excuse for my remarks. I then offered to apologize personally to the woman I had offended. Seeing the look of relief on his face, I realized that, even though the woman I had offended was the aggrieved party, from where my boss was sitting, she had brought him a problem and I had brought him a solution!

I cannot defend my actions in this situation prior to the point where I apologized, but it taught me a lesson. If I look at organizational behavior in terms of justice, she was wronged and got the vindication she deserved. But if I look at it in terms of tribal relations with management, she made herself a problem and I brought a solution. That is what we want to be seen as by our colleagues and our bosses—solutions.

Summing Up

We have a right to expect work to be a source of positive meaning in our lives, but we need to take a balanced view of how much to expect in this regard. Sergeant Majors seldom care too little, but often care too much. When we seek meaning in work and work does not reciprocate, it generally leads to anger or, worse, to tuning out and becoming a zombie. It is important to review the sources of meaning in our life and to assess whether work is in the proper place. In order to achieve a balanced perspective, we must deal with our anger. Anger can be an important diagnostic tool leading us to a large number of ways to be more organizationally effective by identifying and dealing with our anger. Hopefully, the end result of these efforts will be both greater personal satisfaction and more productive work relationships.

CHAPTER 7:
BUILDING POSITIVE CAREER RELATIONSHIPS

When teaching business strategy, I have often lectured to students that if your only strategy is to make a pile of money, you're very unlikely to make much money. Of course you want to make money in business; but if you want profit, you have to focus on creating value for customers. If you do this well, the money will be a by-product. Similarly Sergeant Majors tend to look for meaning at work in the form of successful tasks or projects. There is nothing wrong with this either, but if you want successful outcomes, you can't focus directly on getting there. You have to focus on building the positive relationships that take you there as a group. Remember, the tribal organization does not exist primarily in roles or tasks, but in relationships.

Should and Deserve

Many Sergeant Majors who undervalue the power of relationships rely insistently on what "should" happen. People "should" be using the new procedure because I sent the memo outlining it. The customer service staff "should" check with the warehouse before promising delivery of goods. Workers "should" be happy with their new wage contract. When "should" is directed back at the speaker it becomes "deserve". I deserve that sales management position in

Dallas. My team deserves credit for the recent increase in sales. I deserve better people than this motley team.

"Should" and "deserve" are forms of magical thinking, fantasies that help us defend staying within our comfort zone instead of dealing with the messy relationships that stand in the way of working effectively. When I am consulting to organizations I encourage people to avoid both words. They may have a place in ethics, philosophy or religion, but they do not help us to manage our work affairs.

Nothing in any organization has ever happened because it should.

Nobody gets a reward simply because they deserve it.

Your say your managers *should* appreciate everything you do for the company and you *deserve* a raise or advancement? Maybe you're right. So what? When you are thinking in should-terms and deserve-terms, you are not engaged with the how-questions that matter. *How* will you see that you are appreciated and rewarded? This is a more useful question, one that facilitates problem solving instead of brooding. *How* will you get ahead? Through positive relationships.

You will get ahead when the people who count want you to get ahead, not when you "deserve" to.

Winning Friends; Influencing People

The foundational book on work relationships is Dale Carnegie's *How to Win Friends and Influence People*. After seventy years in print, this book has sold well over thirty million copies. To the cynic, it may seem corny and mindlessly optimistic, but it has spoken to four generations of businesspeople (by the way, make sure you get the revised edition, 1981, as some of the original examples used by Carnegie embody 1930s attitudes that are today seen as racist or sexist).

While Carnegie's message is broadly useful, it has special resonance for us Sergeant Majors. We tend to treat personal relationships as something that can be separated from the "real" work. When we like somebody or we see a connection as vital, we put positive work into the relationship. When we dislike somebody or when we see no payoff, we tend to believe we can ignore the relationship or let it fester, without damaging ourselves. We can't. Here is one of my more painful examples.

Some time ago I worked on a large consulting project. The prominent sociologist Arlie Hochschild was on its advisory committee. I desperately wanted to meet her, but lacked a connection to her. One night, a friend invited me to a conference event being held at a downtown hotel where Hochschild was the main speaker. I jumped at the chance to attend. On the way up to the ballroom, I was one of five people milling about waiting for the elevator and making small talk, as one does, to fill the awkward time. On the edge of the group I saw a woman making the eye and body movements one makes when one wants to join a conversation. I could easily have said something to her, but, as I wasn't looking directly at her, I could also ignore her without appearing rude. I didn't want to make the effort, so I ignored her. The elevator finally arrived and we all got off at the ballroom level. Most of us found a seat in the hall, but the woman I had ignored walked straight to the stage and mounted the podium. Yes, I had snubbed Arlie Hochschild, the very person I was dying to meet!

Many of the relationships which help us in our career are based on something other than the work itself. In addition, many of the relationships which hurt us in our careers either do not directly involve us or take place out of our presence. We may even be hurt, not by negative relationships, but by an absence of relationships.

When the senior managers got together to discuss candidates for running the new Beijing office, our name just didn't come up. When we learned that the person who would head this office was Brian, a team leader we thought to be mediocre, but who plays on the company softball team and who organized the karaoke and Secret Santa events at the Christmas party, we dismissed it all as brown nosing—and worse. The fact of the matter is, though, that whether the relationships which put Brian into his new role are legitimate or not—that is how he got there! Brian got noticed and we did not. If we wish to build the relationships that permit us to thrive in the organization, we need to get past "should" and "deserve" to ask how these relationships *do* work.

Impoverished Networks
Up to a point, Sergeant Majors do create positive relationship networks, but we tend not to create relationships we regard as superfluous or insincere, so our networks are thin, impoverished. This is a disadvantage.

- Why should I make peace with Tom? He's a jerk and a troublemaker. Besides, we're in the same job. I don't need to answer to him.

- I suppose I should go into the plant more often to spend time with the production people. After all, we have to coordinate schedules with them. But I'm up to my ears in real work. I can't be bothered to stand around bullshitting. Besides, I don't have much in common with them.

- No, I'm not going to the company picnic. First I'd have to show how bad a softball player I am, then I'd have to listen to the damned karaoke Brian's committee is arranging. It's not worth it for a couple free beers. Besides, I have to work Saturday to make sure the new release is ready for Monday morning.

In the last of these points, note that we think we're even prioritizing the company's interest over our own. While Brian is singing an off-key version of My Way, we're sweating to make sure the new release is bulletproof. That's what matters, right? Maybe it "should"—but it doesn't.

Remember, Brian put in a full work week too. It's only in our judgment that his commitment is deficient. By sweating away on Saturday, we're reinforcing a boundary between ourselves and everyone at the picnic, who all seem to think Saturday should be fun. In contrast to our self-imposed martyrdom, Brian made himself visible to everyone and did so in a positive way. Even when he embarrassed himself singing My Way, it strengthened his relationships with the crowd. Being able to share a laugh at your own expense is endearing; it brought him closer to everyone. Makes you shudder, doesn't it? Sorry, I don't get to make the rules.

Neither do you.

Over time, Brian's network of relationships will be much richer than those of a Sergeant Major. We will have a minimal network composed of those we like and those we can see as useful. To us, this seems enough; it isn't. Brian's network contains everyone he meets—period. Where Brian has a huge advantage is that none of us knows which relationships will be useful. Over the course of Brian's career, much of the advantage that comes to him will be from unexpected sources. An old fraternity buddy will become a major client. Somebody he made a good impression on when they were nobody will return as the chief financial officer. A key person will sign onto Brian's team because his wife was the star shortstop on Brian's softball team. As Sergeant Majors, we need to stop calling this inappropriate. It is not inappropriate. It is tribal. It is human.

Building Quality Relationships

Having a network containing too few relationships is just one problem we are likely to encounter as Sergeant Majors. We also have to look at the quality of our relationships. In chapter eight, we will consider how to influence these relationships productively, but first it is necessary to understand how to build a quality relationship network. The remainder of this chapter will consider two points: building adult-to-adult relationships and nonverbal communication. Both are essential relationship-building tools and both are likely pitfalls for a Sergeant Major.

Adult to Adult Relationships
Most organizational relationships function best as peer relationships. Even between levels of authority, the team leader and the CEO are peers in the sense that they are both mature, adult people. In contrast, Sergeant Majors tend to often think in terms of top-down

and bottom-up relationships. We ascribe powers to our boss that our boss doesn't have. We look down on those we disrespect rather than being able to see them as peers. If we look at anybody who is fitting in well and advancing or thriving in our organization, we are likely to find that they have a great many adult-adult relationships and relatively few top-bottom ones.

A useful way to think about this comes from transactional analysis, a psychological framework developed by Eric Berne and popular for a half century. There are several good texts and online resources for anyone interested in a more detailed understanding of this theory.

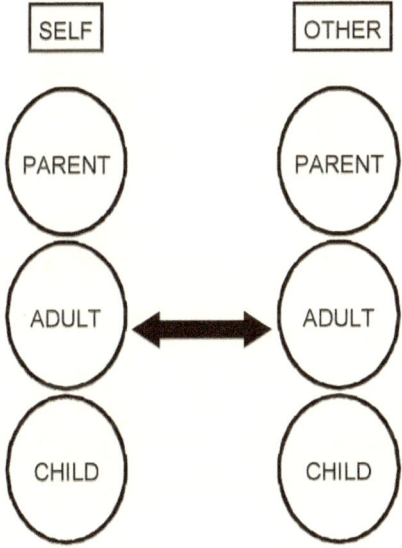

Berne was interested in the mental states we assume when we interact with others. When we are in the **Parent** state, we act the way we experienced parental figures acting toward us as children. In the **Child** state, we respond as children. Perhaps the Parent scolds and the Child reacts with shame or anger. In between the Parent and Child states is the **Adult** state, in which we use all of our mature resources to interact as peers. This simple model can be very useful for understanding the types of interactions we are having with others at work.

In general, we will find that taking the parent or the child role is unhelpful to us in the workplace. That does not mean we haven't had good reasons to follow bad role models in this respect. Our earliest employment, if we had hourly, part-time work, probably followed a parent-child model of management. We were patted on the head when we did what we were told and threatened or punished when we did not.

Historically, factory work and the military have also followed this model and it is still influential (even though, for at least three decades, the most advanced factories and armies have been moving in the direction of more adult-adult work relationships). It is a safe assumption for the Sergeant Major that any time I find I am taking the parent or the child role, I should stop, look at what I am doing, and change how I am interacting. Here are a couple examples

Adult to child:
> "You promised to take care of that report and you didn't. Now I have a problem and that makes me your problem. Fix this and I don't want to have this conversation with you again!"

Reframing as Adult to Adult:
> *"We have a problem because the information from that report didn't get to Corporate. Let's take a few minutes to figure out how to get ourselves out of this problem and keep it from happening again."*

Child to Adult:
> Pat is a jerk. I skip her meetings whenever possible, participate as little as I can when I have to attend and I try not to have to speak to her in the halls.

Reframing as Adult to Adult:
> *Because Pat and I have a bad history, I make a special effort to be friendly and ask about things at work and home. I go out of my way to find out why we had difficulties and to work with Pat to make sure these negative feelings don't escalate.*

As Sergeant Majors, we are especially prone to taking the child or the adult role in three types of relationships: interacting as children with our bosses, interacting as parents with our employees, and interacting either as parents or children with those who cross us.

Our Bosses Are Not Our Parents.

Yes, our bosses are authority figures and we must respect that, but their authority is not parental. They are not more highly developed human beings. They are simply people in a different role. I mentioned in chapter two that we tend to treat our bosses as if they were omniscient, just because they have authority in our area. We also tend to take their judgments as dictates. Rather than dealing subserviently with people up the ladder from us, it can be more helpful to interact as one mature person to another. This involves making casual conversation, recognizing the limits of their knowledge and acting as we would with a peer to help them in their job, to the extent that it is related to ours. Organizational children are never promoted to adult. That transformation is entirely up to us.

We Are Not Our Employees' Parents.

Many Sergeant Majors become well regarded team leaders because we tend to genuinely care for "our" people and to be willing to go to bat for them. This can be taken too far, though. They are not "ours". They are people who work with us in one of their several life roles. Beyond the work task, we cannot take care of them and it is not our place to do so. We can refer the worker with a drug problem to human resources, but we are not the ones who can help him get clean. We can be understanding to the worker who has an abusive husband when she is chronically late or "sick", but we cannot fix her home life. We might want to teach a lesson to that racist sales manager who talked down to our black project leader at the sales meeting and embarrassed him inappropriately—but before picking up our flaming sword, we have to ask what an adult-adult way of dealing with this situation would be.

Engaging as an Adult

When I had my cafes, I was once travelling to a trade show with my manager when she told me about sixteen year old Dana, one of our best employees, being expelled from school. As it was told to me, Dana was necking with her girlfriend in the halls in a manner quite common to the heterosexual students, when she was pulled into the principal's office and expelled. To add insult to injury, her mother learned that her daughter was in a lesbian relationship by getting a call from the assistant principal. As a consequence, Dana was grounded. I was furious, but, fortunately, I was also out of town and helpless. During the next two days, I planned all sorts of adult-child retribution. I thought of calling the school, chatting to Dana's mother, writing to the local newspaper. Common to all of these ideas was my intention of *punishing* those I saw as wrongdoers. That would not have been constructive and it was none of my business to do so. In the end, we decided to have a party for Dana to show our support for her and whatever life choices she decided to make. She was thrilled; we had done what we could and there was no Sergeant-Major collateral damage to clean up afterward.

Engaging as an adult is difficult. It often means being the first to put aside anger or hurt feelings. It means not seeing the other person as a villain. It means accepting that we will not be vindicated as having been wronged. It means accepting limits to our ability to influence what we care about. When you come right down to it, isn't this largely what maturity is about? As adults, we do not learn to feel less passionately than we did as children. We just learn that when five year old Britney screams, "I hate you, I hate you", we enforce healthy boundaries and respond without anger, no matter what we are feeling.

Becoming aware of the difficulty we experience when moving from child or parent roles to adult roles can help us to better sympathize with what the other person we are dealing with is going through. Their emotional responses to conflict are probably not greatly different from ours. While our minds are busily trying to defend our ego, theirs is doing the same thing. If we are to move into constructive relationships, we have to stop this mutual defensiveness—and it usually has to start with us. Moving to adult-adult relationships will generally involve a period of dealing with an adult-parent or adult-child relationship. If you give in to the temptation to respond in kind, things will deteriorate. If you persist in interacting as an adult, it is surprising how often you will find the other person responding in kind.

MANAGING ADULT-ADULT RELATIONSHIPS

It can help you to reflect on your work relationships if you keep a log of your conflicts. If you like, you can think back to prior conflicts. One way to do this is to identify everyone at work who you dislike and ask yourself how you came to dislike them. In each situation, use the Transactional Analysis model to ask:

- Does Parent, Adult or Child best describe my position in this conflict?

- Does Parent, Adult or Child best describe the other person's position?

- If everything is Adult-Adult, pat yourself on the back and stop. If not:

- How does my Parent (or Child) behaviour produce Child (or Parent) behaviour in the other person?

- What examples of Adult behaviour can I think of? Make a list.

- How can (could) I use these examples to move this conflict to an Adult-Adult frame?

Nonverbal Communication

Communication is the main way one manages relationships.

Relationships determine your standing in the tribal organization.

The tribal organization determines your future.

Some experts believe as little as 10% of communication is verbal.

What was that last one?

That's right. If you've only been watching what you said or what you wrote at work, you have hardly been watching your communication at all. In a court of law, you would have a defense: Nothing in the memo actually *says* that you think the new project is a waste of money or that the project leader is an idiot. Acquitted! But you are not in a court of law; you are in a tribe. What have you been communicating to your tribe about the project and its leaders?

Well, your non-attendance at those "stupid" meetings was noticed. So is your nonparticipation in conversations about the project. The face you make whenever somebody mentions that project speaks volumes. Oppressed people everywhere are expert at conveying their message without actually saying it and Sergeant Majors often think like oppressed people. Nonverbal communication may be accurate or inaccurate, positive or negative. You don't have to try to stop communicating nonverbally—nor could you. You do have to be aware of what you are communicating and learn to use it positively.

It may help to think about how you experience nonverbal communication from others. Think about that project leader who can't stand you or the employee you think is totally unmotivated. Think about that sales presentation you did where the audience had no interest in the product and was there only because their boss demanded it. In all of these cases, don't you sense the negative feelings clearly, regardless of whether they are stated? What cues do you pick up on?

- Facial expressions, eyes staring at the floor, ceiling or anything but you.

- Body language, crossed arms, inattentive positions.

- Notebooks are closed. Pens are in pockets.

- The tone of what is said, sarcastic inflections, etc.

- Lack of participation.

- Finding that wherever you lead the conversation, it goes someplace else.

- The absence of meaningless pleasantries. Nobody asks you about the weather, the big game last night or how your hotel is.

- Lack of conversation as everyone leaves at the conclusion of your presentation (and not a moment later).

Without saying an untoward word, people can make a situation like that unbearable. Although they can say they cooperated with you, it is palpably clear to you that they are fighting you every step of the way and you, justifiably, hate it. Now be honest, have you ever done this to somebody else expecting not to be noticed? I'll bet you have.

Dress and Environment

What are you communicating in the way you dress? Did you wear your Green Day T-shirt to the barbecue with the sales team, just to show you weren't one of "the suits". Well, you made your point. Should you have? I was once hired in an academic department as the most senior person and I was told that a reason for my being hired was for me to be a mentor to junior staff. I began my career with that organization dressing highly professionally and a bit ahead of the departmental norm, as befits a mentor. As I learned that I actually had no such role in the department and became progressively more alienated and negative, my dress standard fell until, on a bad day, I looked like a transient living out of a duffle bag. None of this was against any explicit dress code, but a sensitive observer could have dependably worked out my attitude just from the way I dressed for work.

Almost any way that clothing can be noticed is negative. In a work setting, if it is noticed, it is noticed as too expensive (has another income?), too cheap (doesn't care or has financial problems?), too stylish (adolescent?), too revealing (inappropriately sexual?). Whether you work in a company logo shirt, casual dress or a suit, the highest compliment you can receive is not to be noticed for your dress. When it is not noticed, it fits in. When you fit in, you are managing tribal relationships.

Let's look at your office. Does the level of organization and cleanliness look professional? What's that written on your coffee cup? Maybe you want to put that away and take out the one you were given to celebrate the recent merger. Is there music playing? Bach? Madonna? Coldplay? What does it say about you? Most importantly, how consistent is it with the tribal culture that you want to be part of? What cards, signs and graffiti do you have posted? Do they identify you as part of the group or as somebody standing outside the group criticizing it? How about your other artifacts? What different messages are sent by a framed picture of the wife and kids, a poster advocating gay rights and a Han Solo action figure on your desk?

You can also arrange these nonverbal messages in a positive way. I have often had people comment that my office feels friendly and home-like to them. That has come from my accumulating things that are personally meaningful to me. From the throw rug to the paper maché parrot, the career awards and degrees to the old posters; everything has a story and the stories add up to me. The nonverbal message these items send helps people to better understand and appreciate me.

On the other hand, it would be a good idea to take the quote from Thoreau off my door which reads, "The ways by which you may get money almost without exception lead downward." That's the kind of thing that a Sergeant Major does to say, "I'm not a part of this group; I'm in opposition". It also tends to say "I think I'm better than you."

Managing Nonverbals Starts With Awareness
Because we tend to be largely unaware of the nonverbal messages we are sending, we cannot manage them. What's the use pretending to get along with the company receptionist if your nonverbals say, "I don't respect you"? To make matters worse, our unconscious nonverbal messages tend to be sincere, which makes them hard to retract. To get into the habit of thinking about your nonverbals and making them something you can manage, use the following list to tabulate the nonverbal messages you are sending. You can think back on incidents from the past or use this list as events occur. The important thing is to practice.

WHAT NONVERBAL MESSAGES DID I SEND?

- Facial expressions
- Posture
- Phrasing of my language
- Tone of my language
- What I did NOT do: (chat, attend meetings…)
- Clothing
- Smiling
- Laughter
- Listening – or not
- Artifacts in my office or elsewhere
- Choice of communication media, *i.e.* email instead of personal
- What else can you think of?

Summing Up

Finding meaning in our work lives cannot come directly from successfully performing tasks. In order to be successful in the tasks, we must build a network of positive relationships. It is this network, an element of the tribal organization, that will largely determine our opportunities and our ability to reach goals. If we wish to improve our relationship network, we must spend less time thinking about what "should" happen and more time trying to understand how things *do* happen. One important skill to work on in building relationships is learning to engage in positive, adult-adult relationships with others rather than taking unproductive parent or child roles. A second important skill is becoming conscious of our nonverbal communication and learning to send the message we want to convey rather than the message we think we are keeping secret. Once we have become comfortable working with our network of relationships, it is time to mobilize them as we market ourselves. That is the subject of the next chapter.

CHAPTER 8:
MARKETING YOURSELF

⌒*ᴍ*⌒

T he main point I have been trying to convey in the previous three chapters is that your career is not something that is built on a succession of completed tasks. It is something that grows within a network of positive relationships. If you grasp this point and are beginning to better understand how these relationships affect you, it is time to start thinking about what you can do within this network to achieve the career you want.

You have value that can benefit your organization and, since starting this book, you have learned ways to increase that value. How do you get it recognized? Fortunately, there is a discipline whose central question is how to connect things of value with those who value them: marketing. In this chapter I will explain how you can better learn to promote yourself by applying some time-tested principles from marketing. Here are the main points to consider:

You are a product, or at least your career is.

You need a marketing plan for this product.

You must become a salesperson—don't panic; bear with me.

A good salesperson follows a specific process that can benefit you.

You as a Product

It may seem a bit cold to call your career a product. Okay, try to imagine how you would look to a head-hunter. To a straight-commission recruiter, a product is exactly what you are. How would she see you? What can this product do? Where is the value? Try to look at yourself as dispassionately as you would shop for a new TV. What unique capabilities does it have? Who values those features? Remember what the market does to generic products—they are discounted, discounted again, then discontinued. You don't want that.

If you have been humming along doing your job and expecting advancement, you have implicitly been treating your performance on that job as the only feature of the product. The problem with this is that nobody else has the perspective on your work that you do. You think your performance forms a complete description of your ability and potential because you spend your entire workday with yourself. You know everything you do. How much of that gets seen by those who matter in advancing your career? Even your immediate boss probably sees only a tiny fraction of your work life.

Bureaucratic Value ≠ Tribal Value

Your "product" has two groups of features. One is you as you appear in your personnel file and formal company records of the bureaucratic organization. The other is the you that appears in the tribal relationships that can influence your career. First, think about how little your bureaucratic file shows about you.

I have hired or participated in the hiring of many people, both as a manager and as an employer. Whether hiring hourly workers or professionals, it is amazing how little you learn about a person from their files. Once you start looking at, say, the top third of applicants, everybody has a resume that appears to show the right qualifications. Everyone has reference letters saying they can turn water into wine. Everyone looks appropriate in their interview. Everyone has read the how-to-get-a-job books and knows the expected answer to the interview questions. At best, you can distinguish somebody who is at least marginally qualified from somebody who is not.

That has been the flaw in your logic if you thought doing the job well would lead to advancement. You need to do your job adequately well, but exceptional performance is mostly irrelevant to advancement. Okay, you were in the 15% who got a raise last year because you "exceeded expectations". So what? Remember what I said about school reality and work reality in chapter three? Out here, nobody knows the difference between the student who scored 94 and the one who scored 89. That is why you need to focus on the other side of your product portfolio—your value in the tribal organization.

The most fundamental point to remember about your value to the tribal organization is that your value is determined entirely by the perceptions of others. There is no point railing that you're a valuable person and nobody appreciates it. You are not valuable unless somebody values it. This doesn't mean that objective factors are completely irrelevant. People often appreciate a dependable performer. They tend to remember favors. They like people who are likeable. All of these things have an objective aspect. My point is that neither you nor any objective authority has a voice in determining your value. You *have* value to the extent that you *are* valued—period.

The Four Ps of Marketing Yourself

What would a marketing plan consist of? Well, if you think of your career as a product, you need to promote positive brand awareness of that product. To do that, you want to think of what are referred to as the four Ps in marketing:

The Four Ps

1. Product
2. Pricing
3. Placement
4. Promotion

Product:
The first thing one needs for a successful marketing plan is a product to market. Most of this book so far has been about how you can add value to your product. But this only returns you to the initial problem: Why isn't your product more highly valued than it is?

Pricing:
We can think of your salary, benefits and quality of work life as the "price" your product brings in the marketplace. Remember to think in terms of the total value you receive and not just money. This is true of any product. What is purchased is a bundle of benefits and what is given in exchange is a variety of compensations. For instance, when I was in business, I paid my suppliers cash, but I also gave them loyalty, constructive feedback, referrals...many forms of non-cash compensation. What I purchased was not just coffee, fruit or advertising services, but dependability, quality, flexibility... another bundle of features.

One person looking at their career might see a higher paying job as being the key part of the pricing package she values. Another person might accept less salary in order to have more family time, or to live in Honolulu. Still another might prefer to add worklife quality to his present position rather than to "advance." On both the supply and the demand side, get used to thinking about the product and the compensation as a bundle of features.

Pricing is not something you can directly control in your marketing plan. The market determines value. You can look at the value you have as a reflection of the success of your marketing plan. Your price is both the goal and a diagnostic tool. It is the goal in the sense that if you achieve all of the compensations that are important to you, you have reached your career goal. Until that point, the difference between what you have and what you want is an accurate measure of the difference between the value you wish to supply and the value the market places on you. If you are not receiving the value you want, there are only two possible things to be working on. Either you need to increase the value you are providing or you need to more successfully market the value you have.

Placement:

Effective placement means getting the product to the potential customer in a way that makes the customer realize its value. This is extremely important to you, both because it is essential and because a Sergeant Major is likely to give it little attention.

Ask yourself why a simple product like Coca Cola occupies half an aisle in the supermarket when a much smaller display would do. This is about placing the product in front of the customer. By making different sizes, different packaging combinations, cans and bottles, low-sugar, diet, caffeine-free, cherry, and whatever else they can think of, the company creates a product line that fills a huge amount of shelf space. That, in turn, makes it more likely you'll notice the display and pick something up during the long walk past.

You aren't a bottle of Coke, but you face the same challenge. Who are your "customers"—the people who will make the decisions that influence your career? Is your product in front of them? You may have performed brilliantly in your work team all year, but if all senior management saw of you in addition to your annual performance evaluation was your slightly inebriated and incoherent toast at the Christmas party, you have some work to do to improve the placement of your product.

A good first step is to *not* display the product's weaknesses. Cigarettes are not advertised as "high in nicotine" and you should not have advertised that you were not in full control of yourself at the party. That flaming e-mail about the strategy of developing an office in China advertised the negative features of your product. So did your sullen behavior at that meeting with "the idiot from corporate."

Of course, hiding your weaknesses is not enough. Your assets have to reach the customer's attention. Don't just think about how to make your work more visible. Think about how to show other assets: friendliness, humor, social grace, a good fit with the company's culture, support for company values and objectives. To repeat: your product is a bundle of abilities and behaviors. It is much broader than just your task performance.

Here is an exercise that can help you develop a clearer idea of how you are succeeding at product placement and where you need to do additional work:

PLACING MY "PRODUCT"

- Make a list of everyone who might be a "customer", that is, anyone who has a role in determining your career success. For each person list a name and a role, for instance: Deneise Walker; Purchasing Manager.

- Once you have the list, add a third item: How is this person a potential customer, that is, how can they help or hurt your career? For instance, "Highly visible to senior management; the people she speaks well of tend to get ahead."

- On a separate page for each person make two lists.

  1. First, in their *role* what are the positive and negative things you do (or can do) to influence their perception of you in the relationship between your *role* and theirs.

  2. Second – and this is the list you may have given less attention to – what are the positive and negative things you do (or can do) that influence the relationship between the two of you *as people*. Perhaps Margaret is a fundamentalist Christian. Asking her about her faith and showing respect for the way it influences her life and work is a positive. Arguing with her about the theory of evolution is probably a negative. Remember:

     We are not rational creatures whose feelings sometimes interfere with our objectivity. We are emotional creatures who occasionally supplement our feelings with objective information.

- Once you have these two lists, you know what you are presently delivering to the customer and can assess how well it fits with what you want to deliver. If you are being thorough and honest with yourself, there will be many places where you are delivering a product with the wrong features. There will be other places where you need to deliver the product where there is presently no delivery at all.

Now, what are you going to do to improve your product placement? The essential challenge is one of "product fit." That is, the needs of the customer should match the features of the product. You can work on changing either or both. You can change the bundle of assets you bring to the table by taking training courses or by changing your behavior. You can try to better understand the needs of the customer or help that person better see what value you offer. You are likely to need to do some of both. In the end, your success will be determined how well what you offer is matched to what they think they want.

Promotion:

The fourth "P" is promotion, basically, selling the product to the customer. If you are a Sergeant Major plateaued in a sales position, you have an advantage; you already see yourself as a salesperson. For the rest of us, the notion of sales probably sounds threatening and unpalatable in about equal measure. If it is threatening, we need to recognize that selling, while challenging, is not magic. There are concrete tasks we can work on to become better at this process. If it is unpalatable, that may be because we need to better understand the difference between effective selling and the stereotypes we may have gotten from encounters with telemarketers and used car salespeople.

Becoming a Salesperson: Selling Up, Not "Selling Out"

Many of us became Sergeant Majors, in part, because we were determined to make a living without selling our souls. Ironically, many of us found ourselves in soul-destroying work situations. If "selling" sounds like "selling out" to you, it is important to reframe the way you look at the situation. People who are not in sales often confuse good selling with the ability to sell "ice cubes to Eskimos". This is precisely wrong. Good selling is based on finding a legitimate match between a customer need and a product, then communicating that match to the customer. If you still have reservations, consider this:

You have been selling yourself right along; you've just been doing it badly.

Every contact we have with somebody puts our "product" in front of a customer. You made a successful sales pitch on your job interview and, since then, you have been making a sale with every paycheck you cashed. Since the product you're selling is nothing less than your very life, isn't it a good idea to think a bit about how to do this as effectively as possible?

The blueprint for selling yourself as a product is Dale Carnegie's *How to Win Friends and Influence People.* The simple premise of this book, which has more than demonstrated its effectiveness, is that success is largely determined by one's ability to influence interpersonal relationships. It is significant that the title of this book is not about how to control people or how to manipulate people. Neither control nor manipulation can be successful in the long run. You can, though, learn to influence outcomes. Don't mistake these efforts for a mere exercise in appearance management. To a large extent, the value of your relationship network will depend on the authenticity of your relationships.

Several years ago I needed to buy a car in Los Angeles. Throughout the course of a very long day I dealt with perhaps a dozen of the lowest form of auto-sales predators. Their questions made it apparent that they were working from their need to make a commission rather than my needs as a driver. The most revealing question they asked was, "How much do you want to spend on a car?" Like most buyers, I don't *want* to spend money. I want to find features that match my needs, then spend as little as possible! One guy even responded to my question about a sunroof by saying, without checking, "They don't make them in that model." Yes they do; I had driven one earlier that day at another dealership!

Late in the day I drove an hour and a half across the hell of LA rush hour to return to the first person I had spoken to that morning. He could not offer me a better car or a better price, but he had been the one person who had treated the sales process as one of trying to learn what I needed, then seeing how he could fill that need. Not only did I buy from him, I asked to see the sales manager so I could explain why I had gone out of my way to purchase from his company. That is an example of the kind of selling you want to learn to do.

Developing Your Plan

If you want to be effective in selling yourself, your marketing plan should cover six areas:

1. Have a product that you believe in
2. Find the customer, learn their needs
3. Find the decision maker
4. Surface and respond to objections
5. "Close" the sale
6. Build an ongoing relationship

Product

I have talked about your career as a product. Is it a product you can believe in? Selling yourself isn't about getting special advantage or consideration. It's about getting the recognition you have earned. To earn career advancement, you need to have produced a product with customer value. Wanting advancement isn't a valid reason for your product to sell. Have you made sure you believe in your product for the one valid reason—that you have value to offer?

Don't confuse the product of your work with the product we are discussing, which is your career. You may hold three patents on equipment you developed. You may have tripled sales of your company's brand in your regional market. Maybe you rationalized and streamlined the financial reporting of your company. That's not the product. It's a product feature. It shows something you have done. What else have you done? What can you do? What is your standing in the tribal organization? The product we are talking about is you, all of you. What value does that have? Who values it? Unless you are clear on the product and the customer, it is unlikely your career will follow the trajectory you want.

Customer Needs.

A previous section asked you to identify your customers and their needs. Your sales plan needs to be based on filling those needs. Dale

Carnegie wrote that, although he is very fond of strawberries and cream, he finds fish prefer worms. Therefore, when he goes fishing, he baits his hook with what the fish want, not with what he would like. It's amazing how often most of us offer others strawberries instead of worms. You may wish people valued you more for your technical skills even though they think your social skills are more critical in the position you want. Keep your plan focused to their needs, not the needs you want them to have.

Decision Maker.

There is a certain value to "selling" everyone you meet in terms of making a positive impression, but that is not enough. You have to determine the key people influencing your career and actively show them that your product meets their needs. These people are the decision makers, the gate keepers who will make and influence key decisions about you. Any good sales training course will devote some time to reminding trainees not to waste their time selling somebody who is not the decision maker.

Remember, the gate keeper is not necessarily the person with formal authority over you. The busy boss may delegate a large part of a decision to their administrative assistant, who is closer to the day to day details of issues. A highly placed executive may listen primarily to a golf or gym buddy who deals with your team. Give some thought to who really has influence. Don't blindly assume it is the person who nominally makes the decision.

Surfacing Objections.

In the field of organizational change management, one of the important issues to manage is called "resistance". One gets change to happen by identifying people's resistance and turning it into support. Similarly, a large part of the sales process consists of identifying and overcoming resistance. Imagine a fleet manager being approached by the sales manager at the local Ford dealership:

"So you like our new walk-in cargo vans?"

"They're nice, but we can't afford them."

"You might be surprised that with our new lease plan, these may cost you very little more than those cramped vans you're using now. By the way, how has your fuel budget gone this year?"

"Don't ask! We're more than 50% over budget. That's one reason we have no capital budget for new vans."

"Did you know that these small-displacement diesel engines offer about 30% better fuel economy than your engines? They also have about one-third lower maintenance costs and are projected to last more than 50% longer. The way fuel is going, maybe the question you have to ask is whether you can afford your present vans. What is it that attracts you to these new models?"

"Well, they carry a good deal more than our present vans and our delivery people can get in and out faster because of the high door and headroom."

"Those are two more ways they'd be helping to get your budget back on track. I'm sure your customers would value faster deliveries and fewer special pickup arrangements. That means more business and more loyal customers in the long run. Lets take a minute to look at what we can give you for your old fleet..."

Notice that this salesperson is not operating from her need to earn a commission, but from the customer's need to make deliveries effectively at the lowest cost. The customer has not had his arm twisted, nor has he been sold a bill of goods. Rather, the sales process has used his objections to identify obstacles to the sale and to use these to educate and communicate. The sale is made because the salesperson has shown that the decision to buy the new vans makes good business sense. You can apply all of these lessons to selling your career value.

Your first task is to surface the objection. Commonly, objections are hidden and these can do you great damage. I once had a general manager tell me, with reference to some sarcastic memos I had written, that he "liked a smartass." He said this with a smile, as if it were a compliment. In retrospect, I know it was a flag marking an "objection" I could have done a better job managing. Because his comment was masked as a compliment, I misinterpreted what it meant. If you would like to better understand the ways objections are hidden or deflected, making them hard to identify, I recommend the passages about "managing resistance" in the Peter Block book, *Flawless Consulting*. You will also find sales training materials useful in this regard.

Closing

In sales, closing the deal is what separates winners from losers. In your career, this step is less crucial, but still worth keeping in mind. Are you wondering what career opportunities you may have with this company? Don't wait for things to be given to you. Talk to your boss about it. Talk to people you might work for in other areas about the possibility of transferring to their group. Talk (discretely) to people in other companies, to suppliers, to customers. Remember the cardinal rule of closing a sale: *Ask for the order.* If you want a new position, ask what stands between you and that position. Then manage objections; this means both improving your product and better communicating its features to decision makers—until you have a sale.

Ongoing Relationship

The final point to bear in mind is that a sale is not an event but a moment in an ongoing process. Think like L.L. Bean's, whose motto has long been that a sale is complete only when the product is worn out and the customer is still completely satisfied. Like Bean's, you want to build long-term relationships. When done well, the selling process is ongoing and cyclical. Don't think just about how to get this project completed or how to get that promotion. Think in terms of building the value of your product (your career capital) over the span of your career, both within your company and in terms of capital that is "portable"—that you can sell to another company or use yourself in self-employment.

Getting Feedback

Most of this book has asked you to see yourself, the organization, and your career differently. It has told you to pay attention to relationships you may have given little thought to. In the last couple of chapters, I have been emphasizing that your career value exists only in the perceptions of others. Learning to see and to understand the relationships central to this book will be a challenge for anyone who is a Sergeant Major. That is why the feedback of those you trust is going to be invaluable.

If your critical need is to better understand how others see you, who is in a better position to help you do this that somebody you trust? They do see you as a third party and are going to be a bit more objective about you than you are yourself. Be careful, though. Family tends to see you in terms of the role you had while growing up, not in terms of who you are now. Friends are probably friends because they are similar to you, so they will be likely to overvalue your strengths and undervalue your weaknesses.

Try to triangulate opinions by getting input from people who know you in different capacities. You will, of course, find a variety of conflicting opinions. In all probability, all will have some validity and none will be a perfect picture. Learning to find themes and recognize differences in how these people see you is the best practice you can get in thinking about your career as others see it and not as you want it to be seen.

Sergeant Majors, Dis-missed!

There you have it. Successfully marketing yourself is the final step in moving out of the toxic relationships that constitute the Sergeant Major Syndrome and into a more sustainable and satisfying career.

To review this book in one paragraph: Your career difficulties are not unique. There are millions of us who struggle with them. We are the Sergeant Majors. There are many positive aspects to being a Sergeant Major, but if we are to thrive in our careers, we need to recognize some of the common limitations also. We have most likely learned to be a Sergeant Major by taking bad advice in good faith or taking good advice in directions it was not intended. We can identify these sources and develop a more useful view of work life. We must choose one of three available paths: to thrive as a Sergeant Major, to advance in the organization or to become self-employed. Each of these requires a different strategy, but the same bag of tools can help us to deal with all three. The key goals we must set for ourselves are: managing our anger and frustration; learning to develop and manage a positive network of adult-adult relationships in the tribal, as well as the bureaucratic, organization. Finally, we need to formulate and execute a successful marketing plan for our "product", which is our life, our career.

In the final chapter, my co-author, Mary Hobson, illustrates these points with a story about a Sergeant Major with whom she has worked.

CHAPTER 9:
MY SERGEANT MAJOR

cm

By Mary Hobson

As we have been writing about the Sergeant Major as a metaphor, my mind has returned again and again to an actual Sergeant Major who worked for me in New Zealand. Albert began his career working for a literal Sergeant Major—in the South African army. Since then, he has followed all three of the paths we discuss in chapter five. He appears to have gained something from each of them, and has settled happily into thriving as an organizational Sergeant Major. Albert's story is a good way to illustrate the key points of this book with reference to one individual's career.

I first became Albert's department head at a New Zealand "polytechnic," sort of a trade school blended with a community college. While I later came to value him greatly as a colleague and a department member, my first impression was of his palpably military demeanor. This was not coincidental. Albert's work career began in the South African Army when he was conscripted at age 18. He says it was then that he met one of the greatest influences in his life, Sergeant Major Walker, a career soldier who, during the Second World War, had served as a Sergeant Major in the British army.

Learning from a Real Sergeant Major

Sergeant Major Walker exemplified the qualities we have talked about in this book. On the one hand, he was a highly skilled technician who cared greatly for his team. Albert quite literally owes his life to the skills he learned from this man. He was taught both from the "visible rulebook," things like how to find food in the field under the worst of circumstances and how to survive under fire. He was also taught from the "hidden rulebook" —how to break in a new pair of boots by soaking them in urine, for instance. This was South Africa in the 1970s. That Albert is alive today is a testament to his team leader.

On the other hand, Sergeant Major Walker was not a master of negotiating the relationships of the tribal organization. Although he lived, ate and breathed the army, he seemed to question most of the people in it, except his tribe. To make matters worse, the group he considered to be his tribe changed with circumstances. During everyday life it was his regiment. He treated other units as the enemy and competed against them at all times. When he was on joint army/air force exercises, his tribe expanded to the entire army—against the air force. When he was in combat against another country his tribe was the entire military of his country and the other country was the enemy.

Wartime is one of the few organizational situations in which it is appropriate to see competitors as enemies, but notice how the notion of enemy permeated this man's dealings with others *within* his organization. Albert's early organizational training was based on a world view in which the tribe is beset by enemies. Albert's difficult conscription involved responsibility for people's lives and sometimes their deaths. So when he was honorably discharged, he headed to civilian life with a kick in his step—and his Sergeant Major's lessons well learned.

Encountering the Sergeant Major Syndrome

Albert found a job in what was then the fledgling computing industry, and began the successful early career trajectory characteristic of organizational Sergeant Majors. Through talent and diligence, he progressed from programmer to senior programmer to team leader. He also studied management because, in his mind, he was heading up the ladder to the top. But, despite working for some of the largest multinationals in South Africa, despite helping to develop early computerized financial systems, and despite becoming an advisor on hardware and software systems, Albert plateaued at project manager level. Why?

Albert was good at his job, but had no training in working on his career. The work he did was valuable to the company and he was valued for it, but success in doing the work led to more work of the same kind. The Sergeant Major syndrome was beginning to operate in his career. While his quality was valued, his reputation for taking no bullshit was seen less positively. He did not "suffer fools gladly." His uncompromising attitude meant that although he was recognized as being a valuable technical team leader, he was not going to be promoted into the officer corps. He had hit the Sergeant Major's glass ceiling.

Getting "Ahead" in the Organization

Albert's reaction to hitting the ceiling was unusually insightful and potentially fruitful. Reflecting on the obstacles to his progress, he decided that the path to middle management led through sales. Recognizing that this required developing new skills, he sought a position as a "client liaison," a person responsible for before-and-after sales service. He studied how to sell both his technical product, software systems, and the product discussed in chapter eight himself. He took a position with a different company and he worked on his career as well as his job.

Albert progressed far enough through middle management to be able to see the bottom of senior management. In terms of career progress, he was successful. In personal terms, the results were more mixed. This is why we recommended in chapter five that Sergeant Majors who wish to get "ahead" reflect seriously on whether they want to go there. In the end, Albert didn't fully believe in what he was doing. He was unhappy. He felt that he was finding it necessary to play games with which he was not ethically comfortable. He did not like having to make decisions that were not of direct advantage to his team. "Schmoozing" with other members of the management team was a necessary fact of his work life, but one that often disagreed with him.

The "Freedom" of Self-Employment

At this point, Albert had an opportunity to work as a consultant, along with two other colleagues. Demand was good and the three profited from the venture. While it would never make them rich, it provided a dependable income. In terms of the risk discussed in chapter five, this venture was relatively low risk. The firm needed only a small number of clients and these companies were already quite familiar with Albert and his partners. It was relatively easy to build the client list.

The nature of the business was well suited to three Sergeant Majors in that each of the three principals worked almost independently on a consultancy basis; using each other as support and backup but usually having their own clients. They were able to more or less control their own working world except of course for the bits that were controlled by their clients. This meant that Albert could structure his working environment using his own judgement. In essence, with his ancillary workers, he was able to form his own tribe.

This was a very productive part of Albert's working life. He gained a reputation for excellent technical work. Doing business with him was straightforward because his word was his bond (this is one of the few ways the no-bullshit attitude Sergeant Majors frequently exhibit is seen positively). Due to the quality and dependability of his service, his reputation and his client list grew by word of mouth.

A major part of the work that Albert had ended up with was as a consultant to the South African government working with a UN committee on international financial software standards. This work had limited life, and when it was finished Albert decided that he would pursue a new career, in academia. Faced with the choice of rebuilding his self-employment income or once again becoming an employee, he accepted an opportunity to teach in a South African university, and, in doing so, finally he found a job that he loved.

Thriving as a Sergeant Major

Albert moved to a sister country of his homeland, New Zealand. He was hired by a polytechnic in a small town. Here he made an interesting choice. By now, he had an MBA and a doctorate, which more than qualified him for academic administration—the officer corps—but rather than take a position as manager of the program, Albert chose to be a teacher. Having already succeeded both at getting "ahead" and at being self-employed, Albert had the perspective to make his decision based on knowledge of what he wanted rather than on what he thought he "should" want.

When I first met Albert, I was the new head of his department and he had been at the school for several years. He had apparently been put under some pressure to take the position I had just accepted and it was obvious to anyone who had worked with him that he was more than capable of filling it well. Still, he refused. Albert had been around the block, had succeeded at all three career paths open to a Sergeant Major and he knew what he wanted—to thrive as a Sergeant Major.

Much like a new junior officer who is carried forward by the crusty and experienced "non-com", I was initially senior to Albert in title only. He was the one who had both the knowledge of how things get done and the respect of the troops. He took a very active part in the selection process which led to my appointment, at one point interviewing me by telephone for two hours. His was the last word advising on creating the short list for face to face interviews. He was able to demand and receive a private interview with me, where he would not be disturbed by senior "officers". He insisted I do an impromptu presentation to the entire instructional staff of "his" department. When an administrative problem with human resources threatened to subvert my hiring, it is rumoured that he "taught them a lesson they won't soon forget" and got the matter straightened out. One final stamp of the Sergeant Major was on all of this effort—I didn't know about any of this until more than a year after I took my position!

Albert then began to train me to be his new boss, gently easing me into the job. During the first year he shouldered many of the duties that should have been mine, passing them on bit by bit as I became more familiar with the job. He never forced his opinions on me, but if I asked for advice he was forthcoming, open and honest. I suffered from intermittent ill health at that time, but I quickly learned that if I was down, my Sergeant Major would make sure everything kept going, working in my name and for my interest. He stood behind me to the degree that when I picture Albert in my mind, I see him at attention holding his .303 Enfield rifle, the head of the "thin red line" creating a zone of safety within which I can do my job with peace of mind.

As I became better able to carry the weight of my job, Albert moved willingly into the background, devoting more of his time to teaching and leading his teaching team. He is a very talented teacher and his students love him. In return, he loves the idea of developing the programme that he teaches on. He puts in extra hours of research and development to devise teaching materials that are interesting and informative. He says that he is cheating the institution because he loves what he does so much that he would do it for no pay.

Thriving *With* a Sergeant Major

My relationship with Albert is an example of a key point:

Sergeant Majors are valuable.

It is only the toxic relationships of the Sergeant Major syndrome that we need to avoid.

Working together reveals many things about Albert. We play our roles very well. He is the Sergeant Major to my role as officer. It is his job to make sure that the department functions well. He takes care of the team, maintains discipline in the classroom and across the programmes that he is responsible for. He keeps me well informed, often tells me what I need to do (very gently and often quite respectfully), and is the font of all information, rumor and gossip across the department. Seeing his 6'4" frame at attention outside my door, imaginary Enfield in hand, I do believe he would, if necessary, happily visit physical discomfort on those who would undermine our efforts. So do they!

Albert is happy to leave departmental management to me because the contributions he most wishes to make are elsewhere, at project level. Fancy dinners, diplomacy and what he calls "hair spray events" he willingly avoids. For my part, I see it as my role to protect the boundary within which my Sergeant Major can oversee the internal work of the department. I am a better boundary spanner between the department and everything outside it than is a Sergeant Major. Together, we can work as a team to link project-level work in the department into the complex tribal relationships of the school, the community, our students and government.

Albert exemplifies that oft-quoted verse of T. S. Eliot:

> *The end of all our exploring*
> *Will be to arrive where we started*
> *And to know the place for the first time.*

Because Albert has learned to thrive as a Sergeant Major, he has career satisfaction and our organization is more capable of functioning. In this relationship, there is no trace of the toxic Sergeant Major syndrome. Because Albert has walked in my shoes as a manager, he doesn't dismiss what I do as bullshitting and ass licking. He knows this relationship maintenance needs to be done—even though he hates doing it. Yes, it does often have an unsavoury side, but it is nonetheless necessary and he knows that. He understands that someone else is relieving him of this odious work, allowing him to do what he most cares about—delivering the product.

The other side of the equation is that as Albert's "lieutenant", it is incumbent upon me to give him respect and support. Our relationship cannot be negotiated at my convenience because it is based on respect, trust and commitment—values which cannot be subjected to managerial expediency. Such qualities must always be there or they are not there at all. This limits my ability to make arbitrary and self-interested decisions, but, in terms of building an effective organization, isn't that all to the good? Managing the

Sergeant Major (the subject of our next book), is a challenge, but also a significant benefit. Albert and I support each other because both his role and mine are necessary and because each of us carries some duties the other could not carry without dropping something important. Paradoxically, if each of us gives up something to the other, we both have more than if we did not.

Are You Albert?

I have told a bit of Albert's story because he has taken every path a Sergeant Major can take. He has had a degree of success at all of them. As a result of all this experience, he now knows what he wants, to be valued and valued as a Sergeant Major. Had this been you, the path into middle management might have been the choice that worked best for you. For another person, the self-employment route would have been the way to go. Albert's story should not be interpreted as a lesson that Sergeant Majors are destined to remain Sergeant Majors. The lesson is that we need to both learn the rules and look deep within ourselves so that we can *choose* which path is right for us.

FURTHER READING

This section contains citations or other relevant contact information for the resources mentioned in this book along with a few notes about their connection to *The Sergeant Major Syndrome*. They are arranged by topic.

Bureaucracy

Max Weber, who developed the notion of "bureaucracy", wrote prolifically and in German. The best abridged translation and collection of his work is H. H. Gerth & C. Wright Mills (1946) *From Max Weber: Essays in Sociology*, New York:Oxford University Press. See section VIII entitled, "Bureaucracy."

Company Attitude

Despair.com (http://www.despair.com) is a site dedicated to parody of Successories Inc. (http://www.successories.com) type materials. Any good Sergeant Major will prefer the Despair.com site—and it is important to understand how that is career-limiting.

Giftedness (IQ > 130)

An excellent online introduction to the concept of giftedness is by Stephanie Tolan, a writer who researched the concept in order to better understand her son's giftedness. Start with Discovering the Gifted Ex-Child (http://www.stephanietolan.com/gifted_ex-child.htm). She also has other information available including a bibliography. (http://www.stephanietolan.com/nonfiction.htm).

An excellent counsellor who specializes in assisting gifted, creative and multi-talented adults is Lynne Azpeitia, who also has a web site containing many free resources as well as her contact information for those seeking individualized coaching. We have worked with Lynne and recommend her highly. http://www.gifted-adults.com/content/view/35/62/.

Groups (Dealing with People)
There are two truths about people in organizations that we Sergeant Majors often find hard to accept: (1) People primarily react to their environment, not rationally, but from embedded perceptions, values and feelings; (2) A group is not merely the sum of its members—it has a life of its own. The following are books we have found valuable. There are many, many more from which you can profit.

Wilfred R. Bion (1961/1989) *Experiences in Groups*, London:Tavistock/Routledge. Bion is one of the founders of the study of group dynamics. His book is short and readable. It is, as the title suggests, based on his experiences in dealing with groups, in his case, hospitalized veterans of WW II.

Peter Block (1981/2000) *Flawless Consulting*, New York:Jossey-Bass/Pfeiffer. Don't be misled by the title. Block provides valuable resources in this book for anyone who wants to improve their ability to deal with others in organizations. This book is especially valuable because of its emphasis on dealing with "resistance", the non-rational opposition we encounter when we try to change anything in the workplace. The out-of-print first edition (1981) is a better handbook because it is half the length of the succeeding edition. The second edition is richer in anecdotes and illustrations.

Carnegie, Dale (1936/1981) *How to Win Friends and Influence People*. New York:Pocket Books. Four generations and more than thirty million copies on, Carnegie remains the bible for anyone wanting to better understand and influence their interactions with others. It is a book of tremendous potential value, especially in relationship to what we discuss as selling yourself as a product. Buy the 1981 edition. It has the same lessons as the original, but Carnegie's wife and daughter changed some examples from the original that would be considered offensive today due to changes since the 1930s in prevailing norms about race and gender.

Hidden Rule book

What we call the hidden rule book, Richard Ritti & Steve Levi (2006, *The Ropes to Skip and the Ropes to Know,*7th *ed.*, New York:Wiley) call "the ropes." That this book has reached its seventh edition suggests that it has been found widely useful in helping people learn that there is much more to "knowing the ropes" than just following the rules.

Identity

In chapter 2 we discussed some family role archetypes such as the hero, the Placator and the lost one. The best reference for these is Wayne Kritsberg (1988) *Adult Children of Alcoholics Syndrome: A Step by Step Guide to Discovery and Recovery*, New York:Bantam.

There is a vast literature about gender and work. For those coming to it for the first time, one good introduction is Rosabeth Moss Kanter *(1977/1993) Men and Women of the Corporation*, New York:Basic Books.

Gender, addiction and issues of organizing are all present in Anne Wilson Schaef (1986) *Co-Dependence: Misunderstood, Mistreated*, San Francisco:Harper & Row. Whether male or female, the Sergeant Major is highly prone to co-dependant behaviour and Schaef offers a sympathetic rather than critical perspective on this problem and how to change it. Other fascinating books by Schaef, with co-author Diane Fassel, are

The Addictive Organization and *When Society Becomes an Addict*. Both offer a rich perspective on how an understanding of the distinction between addictive and healthy behaviors can help us to better deal with organizations and social life in general whether we personally suffer from substance dependency problems or not.

Life / Values

We briefly mention Henry David Thoreau's lecture/essay "Life without Principal", which can be found in many places including *Walden & Other Writings* by Henry David Thoreau, J. W. Krutch (ed.) (1962) New York:Bantam. The quote we cite is from p.364 in that edition. In general, Thoreau's readings are a wonderful source of reflection on daily life that can help us to better question who we are and where we want to be heading.

Sergeant Majors, a Cautionary Example

In *The Soul of a New Machine*, Tracy Kidder (1981, New York:Avon) chronicles the efforts of a group of engineers who build a new computer at Data General. We describe this book as a story about a group of Sergeant Majors who are sent on a suicide mission. It is a wonderful parable for those of us who wish to thrive rather than be destroyed by our organizations. The story we cite is from p.224.

Substance Abuse and Recovery

The most successful model for understanding the nature of any compulsive dependency and recovery is that of Alcoholics Anonymous (AA). The 12-step model of AA has so demonstrated its power to change lives that there are presently more than a hundred groups which use this model for narcotics, overeating, gambling and a host of other problems which involve compulsive and damaging behaviors. There are also organizations such as Al Anon that use the model for those who have been hurt by having somebody close to them suffer from an addictive/compulsive problem. Sympathetic advice can be obtained readily and for free by googling local AA or Al Anon volunteers or looking them up in the Yellow Pages.

An excellent book for understanding the general dynamics of addiction and recovery is by Christina Grof (1994) *The Thirst For Wholeness*, New York:Harper Collins. The Schaef and Fassel books mentioned above also provide useful context on this topic.

Transactional Analysis

The principles of transactional analysis are central to our discussion in chapter 7. There are many sources of information available on this topic, but the classic is Eric Berne (1964/1992) *Games People Play: The Basic Handbook of Transactional Analysis*, New York:Ballantine.

Value of M.B.A. (Limiting Belief)

For two generations it has been broadly accepted on faith that the gold standard in management training is the MBA. Recently there has been increasing recognition that what is taught in an MBA program and what is needed in order to manage effectively may not be all that well matched. A good starting point for looking critically at what this degree can and cannot offer you is Henry Mintzberg (2004) *Managers Not MBAs*, San Francisco:Berrett-Kohler

Where "Management" Came from; Where It's Headed

In order to understand how to manage effectively, it is important to understand that although people have been organizing for millennia, what we call "managing" is a way of organizing that is only a little over a century old that emerged mainly from American organizing practices. Roy Jacques (1996) *Manufacturing the Employee*, London:Sage treats this topic in depth. The quote we use is from p.185.

In the last fifteen years, much has been written about post-industrial, postmodern or even post-capitalist management, suggesting that certain tectonic social shifts are underway that will produce something to succeed what we think of as "management". AlvinToffler (1980) *The Third Wave*, New York:Bantam is an accessible and early account of the shape of what these changes may be. Our discussion of the "covert curriculum is based on pp.46-60. For the interested reader, two other insightful texts are Daniel Bell's *The Coming of Post-Industrial Society* and Peter Drucker's *The Age of Discontinuity.*

Open Book Editions
A Berrett-Koehler Partner

Open Book Editions is a joint venture between Berrett-Koehler Publishers and Author Solutions, the market leader in self-publishing. There are many more aspiring authors who share Berrett-Koehler's mission than we can sustainably publish. To serve these authors, Open Book Editions offers a comprehensive self-publishing opportunity.

A Shared Mission

Open Book Editions welcomes authors who share the Berrett-Koehler mission—Creating a World That Works for All. We believe that to truly create a better world, action is needed at all levels—individual, organizational, and societal. At the individual level, our publications help people align their lives with their values and with their aspirations for a better world. At the organizational level, we promote progressive leadership and management practices, socially responsible approaches to business, and humane and effective organizations. At the societal level, we publish content that advances social and economic justice, shared prosperity, sustainability, and new solutions to national and global issues.

Open Book Editions represents a new way to further the BK mission and expand our community. We look forward to helping more authors challenge conventional thinking, introduce new ideas, and foster positive change.

For more information, see the Open Book Editions website:
http://www.iuniverse.com/Packages/OpenBookEditions.aspx

Join the BK Community! See exclusive author videos, join discussion groups, find out about upcoming events, read author blogs, and much more! http://bkcommunity.com/